# WAY TO GO

"SOWING
THE SEED OF BUDDHA"

by

Khentin Tai Situ Pa

edited by Ken Holmes

Published by Kagyu Samye-Ling

Typesetting with the help of Karma Gyurmae, Holland.

ISBN 0 906181 04 6

Bound by Crawford Brothers, Newcastle.


Eskdalemuir,
Nr. Langholm,
Dumfriesshire.
DG13 OQL

CONTENTS

## Guide to the Calligraphies

# Foreword

Although it has become common practice to introduce modern Buddhist books, I hesitate a little, thinking of the simple beauty of traditional Tibetan manuscripts, wherein the meaningful, masterly words of the author are allowed to sparkle and justify themselves, uniquely and indescribably. Those texts, with covers bearing simply a title, treated as treasures wrapped preciously in silks and brocade, have much to teach us, even in their presentation. However, it is highly possible that some readers will not yet have had the opportunity to meet the Khentin Tai Situpa and I am sure that a brief biographical sketch may help them to appreciate the historical and spiritual authority that lies behind the words of advice given in this book.

Our present world belongs to a time dimension known as the 'good kalpa' - 'good' because more than one thousand Buddhas manifest within it. The historical Buddha, Sakyamuni, was the fourth of these and just as he came to this world, led an exemplary life and gave the vast and profound teachings of the universal truths, so also will all the others come and manifest the 'deeds of a Buddha', each coming at a time that is most appropriate in the ever-changing story of the world. The fifth of those Buddhas is called Maitreya and he is at present manifest as the most highly-realized of Bodhisattvas. The Tai Situpa is an emanation of Maitreya. Much can be read of Maitreya in the Mahayana scriptures. He formed part of Lord Buddha's intimate entourage at the time of the main Mahayana teachings on Mt. Gridhrakuta (Vulture Peak) and elsewhere, and one of the two principal traditions of Mahayana transmission stems from him through Acarya Asanga, the other tradition being that of Manjusri Nagarjuna.

Péma Donyö Nyinché Wangpo is the XIIth Tai Situpa, but besides those twelve, mention must be made of those incarnations prior to the first Tai Situpa - as Marpa the Translator, Drogön Réchen, Naljor Yéshé Wangpo and Rigowa Ratnabhadra.

When we look back at the history of Dharma, it hardly seems surprising that the flower of the Buddha's teachings, in its entirety, should have found safe refuge in neighbouring Tibet, and been preserved fully there, whilst it all but disappeared in its native India. However, the debt of gratitude that we owe to the foresight of those early masters who went from Tibet to India, and India to Tibet, during the tenth and eleventh centuries in order to ensure its safe transplantation, is considerable. Of particular note among them was the Tibetan saint Marpa, an emanation of Maitreya and Hévajra. He received the profound instructions of more than one hundred of his most important contemporary Indian Buddhist masters and spent more than sixteen years studying with mahapandita Naropa, one of the very greatest of all Buddhist teachers. Marpa's three journeys to India enabled him to bring back to Tibet the living tradition of all the practices he studied, since he had gained deep spiritual insight into them all. Many are familiar with Marpa through the life-story of his spiritual heir, Milarépa.

Some time after his life as Marpa, he again emanated to form another important link in the Golden Rosary of Kagyu Lamas' (the line of Kagyu Patriarchs) as Drogön Réchen, one of the spiritual heart-sons of Dusum Chenpa, the first Gyalwa Karmapa, from whom he received not only the full responsibility of the Kagyu Patriarchy but also the letter of prediction giving full details of the time and place of incarnation of the second Karmapa. Since the Karmapas were the first Tibetan Lamas to re-emanate in constant succession to continually guide their students, the first tulkus', then this letter was of much historical significance. Drogon Rechen passed the lineage to Gyalse Pomdrakpa who later became the Guru of the second Gyalwa Karmapa, Karma Pakshi.

After his next two incarnations as Naljor Yéshé Wangpo and Rigowa Ratnabhadra, he took birth as Chöji Gyaltsen, a disciple of the fifth Gyalwa Karmapa, Déshin Shekpa, whom he accompanied to China. There Emperor Tai-Ming, who felt a deep respect for him, gave him the title 'Tai Situ'. This was the start of the 'Tai Situ' line of incarnations.

It would be impossible, especially for someone like myself, to attempt to describe the tremendous benefit that the twelve Situ incarnations have brought and are bringing to this world. Great saints, great scholars, great authors, great teachers, great hermits, great Abbots of important monastic institutions and in particular great Gurus, ensuring the full transmission of the Kagyu teachings, especially within the 'Golden Rosary' of Patriarchs, their influence has certainly helped hundreds of thousands of people find the path to truth. One should perhaps give special mention to the fifth Tai Situpa, Chöji Gyaltsen Palzang, since it was he who first received the red Situ crown from Karmapa Wangchuk Dorje; and also Chöji Jungnay, the eighth Tai Situpa, who founded the very important monastery of Palpung, seat of the Situpas and one of the most influential monastic establishments of Tibet. Also that the Situ line is intimately connected with Guru Rinpoché and that it figures in Guru Rinpoché's predictions.

The present Khentin Tai Situpa was recognized and enthroned at Palpung by His Holiness the XVIth Gyalwa Karmapa. In order to set a perfect example for his followers, he studied intensively at Rumtek during his early life, receiving the spiritual transmission directly from His Holiness and the academic transmissions from Khenchen Trangu Rinpoche. He also studied with many of the senior contemporary masters. He is now one of the four Bodhisattva regents maintaining the temporary patriarchy of the Karma Kamtsang tradition until the XVIIth Karmapa takes full office.

Even without these impressive historical credentials, the present Khentin Tai Situpa must be reckoned among the greatest living saints and teachers by his remarkable presence and by the inspiration he gives to those who meet him. With a very evident impartial love, the swiftness of his intelligence and the universality of his approach are a constant reminder that one is in the living presence of Maitreya and Guru Rinpoché, a presence that stays within one afterwards as a spiritual friend for life.

The teachings presented in this book were edited from lectures given by the Tai Situpa in Dublin and Brussels during his 1981 tour of Europe. The spoken word and the written word are different and I hope that in making the transition from one to the other I have not lost that beautiful quality His Eminence has of bringing the Buddha's teaching to life, of making a living breathing landscape from the still-life of the traditional texts; of helping one realize that the Buddha's teaching is always as fresh as if it had been written yesterday, just for you, just for me. The actual subject-matter should be suitable as an introduction to the Buddhadharma for beginners and as a manual of practice for experienced students.

Whilst in a dark and troubled world
Some confused confusing men
Call themselves Maitreya,
Like candles proclaiming themselves the sun,
The genuine warmth and brilliance of your presence
Is awakening in us the forever real,
The power and clarity of your teachings
Is reminding us of the forever true and
The profound vision of your mind
Is guiding us in work of love and peace.

In setting the diamond of your speech,
I hope to have preserved its dazzling sparkle,
That the Buddhas and Bodhisattvas
Will forgive any imperfection or mistake
And that, guided by this wish-fulfilling light
All may eventually come to find, just as it is,
The true and changeless nature of a pure mind.

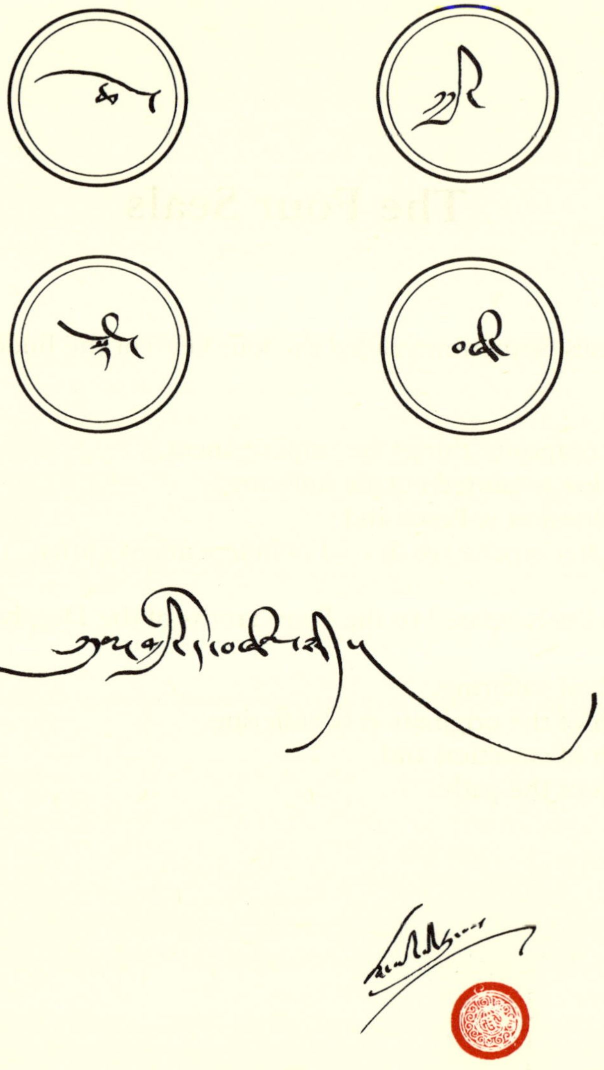

# The Four Seals

The four seals (sometimes called the four keys) of the Buddha's teaching are:

1. that all composite things are impermanent,
2. that all that is tainted entails suffering,
3. that Realization is Peace and
4. that all phenomena are devoid of independent entity.

These are closely related to the Four Truths of the Deeply Realized:

1. the truth of suffering,
2. the truth of the origination of suffering
3. the truth of cessation and
4. the truth of the path.

## 1. All Composite Phenomena Are Impermanent

Anything produced by causes and conditions is impermanent, not only in the sense that it must at some time terminate but also in the sense of its moment-by-moment transformation. The end of birth is death, the end of good is bad, the end of bad is good, the end of togetherness is separation, the end of creation is destruction and the end of composition is decomposition. Because it is always like that, Milarépa says,

*Impermanence, impermanence,*
*There is nothing that has lasting essence!*

Nothing in samsara has a heart, an essence. This is vividly exemplified by the banana tree - when its first skin is peeled away there is another skin, when that skin is peeled there is another, and so on. Eventually one reaches the centre: the tree is hollow - there was nothing more than the skin. In samsara, nothing is any more than illusion and, because it is like that, everything is impermanent yet nevertheless we still see things and then believe in them as 'I' and 'mine'. How the illusion can be taken for real is exemplified by rivers and flames. When we look at the river from a bridge, we see its ripples, current and motion. If we go back the next day, we will see the same thing; even after a year it still looks the same. Actually, since the river is composed of flowing water, it never stays still for even one second and the water we looked at yesterday has long since gone down to the ocean yet we look today and say it is the same river as yesterday. The lamp-flame is dark at its centre, then reddish, then yellow and then again red. It is shaped like an arrow-head. Once again, although it always seems more or less the same, it never does stay the same for even an instant yet we look at it and say 'the' flame. In a similar way to these easy-to-understand examples, everything that we see, hear and feel, is not permanent, even for a second. Moment by moment there is impermanence.

How then should we approach impermanence? Impermanence is not something beyond hope - it is, in fact, full of hope. The Bodhisattva Shantidéva, in his text called the Bodhisattvacaryavatara, says, "...using the vessel of this precious human existence we can cross the mighty river of samsaric suffering". To cross a river we need a boat and to cross samsara's river the precious human existence is the only 'boat' of real use.

Therefore within the impermanence of samsaric illusion, the impermanent but precious human existence is very valuable. Milarépa says, "In life there is no time to be wasted because life is full of destruction". Billions of potentially destructive elements are always awaiting the chance to affect our lives and for that very reason life is said to be like a water-bubble or a lamp in a draughty window - fragile, unpredictable. From the very instant of birth, death has begun and it will be very difficult after death to gain another life like this. The *precious human life* arises as a result of former causes and conditions that were extremely virtuous. Because of that, this life could lead one from suffering to great happiness. It is very valuable but impermanent; easily destroyed. Therefore we should not waste it but make the fullest use of the opportunity and wealth it offers. Not only life, but all things, are impermanent.

## 2. All That Is Tainted Brings Suffering.

There are many ways of understanding this point. Any negative fully-completed (karmically consequential) action is obviously tainted, but even a positive fully-completed action is tainted if it is carried out for selfish motives. More subtly, even positive, fully-completed actions for the benefit of others are tainted if they are accompanied by dualistic thought. The suffering that such tainted actions entail can be approached on many levels. Here we will consider three levels of suffering: 'suffering-suffering', the suffering of change and inherent suffering.

Fully-enacting negative causes will produce suffering-suffering such as birth into the hell-states with their tortures of heat and cold. Fully-enacting positive causes which are selfish will produce the suffering of change, that is, a limited kind of happiness. The happiness is produced by the positiveness of the cause but even if it endures for a million years it must eventually change into suffering. A fully-enacted positive action (even if it is very, very good) that is accompanied by the notion of duality can never lead to final liberation because the seed of suffering, the ego, remains. While that is still there then suffering is inherent, inevitable. How does this seed of suffering work? If we consider the practice of generosity or right conduct, then there is a distinction to be made between generosity and the paramita of generosity; between right conduct and the paramita of right conduct, and so on. Just generosity or just right conduct is good but dualistic - a 'good' opposed to 'bad' wherein the opposite of stealing is generosity and the opposite of lying is to tell the truth. Such goodness is tainted goodness, tainted because there is still some ignorance.

When we talk about ignorance, there is a puzzle to be solved; the puzzle of samsara's origin. Many people ask me the question (which I find very reasonable), "How could samsara have ever begun?" They think this will leave me speechless! But there is much to be said. It is the illusion of ego which is the beginning, the very source of the *twelve links of interdependence.* The first of these links is *ignorance*; ignorance in the sense of not seeing, not knowing, the 'as-it-isness'. That is the beginning of everything. That which is not 'I' is held as 'I'. Since there is no 'I' then there is no 'mine', yet we believe in 'I' and 'mine'.

Everything stems from that point - ignorance. When did it happen? - always, each and every second. Whatever is a pleasant illusion for the 'I', we seek. Whatever is an unpleasant illusion, we try to escape or avoid. In this way, all kinds of subsequent incarnation, the extension of our present existence, are created for us to experience later as results.

The *continuum of incarnation* each minute, each day, each year, becomes incarnation life to life; from human to animal, animal to ghost, ghost to hell, hell to god-realm, god-realm to human and so on. Up to down, down to up, it is always turning like a circle, the circle of the life-dream. Life continues as a circle of reincarnations but the Buddhist teachings will never say that reincarnation, or anything else, has true existence. In that sense, when people say, "There is no good result of virtue...bad result of non-virtue", then I definitely agree. It is so true! But then I must ask the person who says that, "Do you feel happy when things are going well for you? Do you get upset when they go badly? Do you ever make mistakes?" There is only one answer to those questions. The way things appear and the way they really are - are different. We do not yet have enough genuine understanding to see the 'as-it-isness' - the ultimate wherein there is neither happiness nor suffering and likewise no reincarnation. We just see the relative wherein there is happiness and suffering, reincarnation, virtue and non-virtue. It is very simple - they are just there. Reincarnation - the cycle of samsara - is nobody's experience. It is not something created by anybody's will. It is just the experience of *obscured karmic consciousness.* Ignorance was the first link, the perpetual incarnation that it caused was the second link, and now the resultant obscured karmic consciousness is the third link.

Because of that consciousness, good and bad karma will be accumulated. As the universal law of karma is activated, then birth takes place; birth into a specific realm determined by the causes and conditions that have interacted. The specific experiences of that life-situation are also determined by causal conditioning, thus giving the fourth link called *name and form.* 'Name' means communication and 'form' refers to the physical aspect. Mind is joined to body and speech.

Then follows the fifth link: when the karma is fully blossomed there is completion of the *senses.* The degree of completion will depend upon the karma; for instance, those who do not have the karma to possess eye-consciousness will be born blind. Through the completion of the senses there arises the sixth link - *contact* with the various sense-objects. This contact will be either pleasant, unpleasant or neutral. After this arise *feelings* - the seventh link: one detests the unpleasant and appreciates the pleasant, and then there is automatically the eighth link - *attachment.* The attached mind then tries to take or possess the object of its attachment; this *grasping* is the ninth link. Through the taking of what is desired and the rejection of the unwanted, there is the tenth link - *becoming* and this ends in *birth,* the eleventh link. Through birth there is the subsequent *old age and death* and this twelfth link completes the circle. Reincarnation is not something difficult to understand. Yesterday's person and today's person are basically the same and in a similar way, the person of this life and the person of the next life is also basically the same.

Any action which is tainted (whether negative, selfish or dualistic) is not free from the first link, the darkness of ignorance, the notion of 'I'. This is why we say that all that is tainted is suffering. 'Suffering' does not necessarily mean that one's eyes need be full of tears - some people even cry when they are happy! Here 'suffering' covers both suffering itself and the causes of suffering. When explaining this, the Buddha taught that ordinary beings are like the palm of the hand - which cannot feel the touch of a small hair resting upon it. Extraordinary beings are like the eye - sensitive to a hair or even a tiny speck of dust. This means that for ordinary beings duality is not a major issue; we cannot feel the distraction of duality. We can feel the result of duality's negativity, which is like pouring hot water on the palm of the hand but the presence of duality itself is like the hair to which we are insensitive. When we do reach a certain level of realization then the object of our practices, of purification and clarification, is duality itself since it is the seed of all suffering. At that time duality becomes clearly manifest. It can be seen and understood and, like the hair in the eye, clearly felt.

### 3. Realization is Peace:

This is the third seal. 'Realization' does not mean something new or extra. It means *full accumulation* and *full purification.* When there is nothing further to be accumulated or purified, one realizes the ultimate truth, of oneself, by oneself. That understanding is incomparable to any other understanding or realization.

How does such realization come about? It is with us all the time, just as are our own faces. Ignorance is also not something other than us, it is not a new thing. When we realize - that is wisdom. When we do not realize - that is ignorance. One may well wonder, "If this ultimate truth is with us all the time, how is it possible not to realize it?" It is very possible. None of us in all his lives has ever seen his own face. He may have seen a picture or a mirror-image but never directly the face itself. I am twenty-seven and have never seen my face nor will I see it until I die or achieve realization.

The vision of the essence of the mind is obscured by ignorance: because of 'I-and-other' ignorance we cannot see it. When we do first see the nature of the mind we realize that it is something completely other than the self. This is how it is from the first to the tenth profound Bodhisattva levels. The realization at that stage is a subject-object realization and that is the real difference between the Mahabodhisattvas and the Buddhas, because Buddhas' realization completely transcends subject and object. It has nothing at all to do with them. I cannot describe this. No one can describe it. All we can do is actually achieve realization and that in itself is the experience, the explanation and the realization, beyond terminology and duality. All we can say just now is 'realizes itself by itself just as it is'.

How can we start to work towards such realization? Even though everyone has it within, and it is something very absolute, we must start in a very down-to-earth way, on the relative level, by removing the obstacles which block realization - basically desires, aversions and ignorance. Satisfaction is the remover, the purifier, of desire. Loving-kindness is the purifier of anger, and knowledge and wisdom are the purifiers of ignorance.

The understanding of satisfaction has many levels and as one progresses through these levels then desires diminish. Ordinary human nature knows very little satisfaction. A poor person, for instance, may think, "If only I had somewhere to sleep, something to eat and something to wear - that would be quite enough"...but when he actually gets those things then he starts thinking, "Well, this food I have tastes pretty bad - I would prefer something a little tastier. These clothes are so poor - I would like something better to wear. This place where I sleep is so cold - I need somewhere warmer to sleep". So he gets better food, shelter and clothing but still continues thinking, "It's O.K. but I still need more comfortable things". Everything must be bigger and better, and once one has the same as the others in the village, one thinks, "I want to be the best in the village", and once one is the best in the village then, "I must be the best in the whole country" and in this way even if one becomes the richest person in the whole galaxy, the mind is still empty. It is more or less like that for everyone.

Through cultivating satisfaction, loving-kindness and knowledge and wisdom, we need to purify and remove all the obstacles on a very down-to-earth level dealing with them one by one, step by step, until we are free of suffering-suffering, the sufferings of change and the inevitable suffering, truly ridding ourselves of duality, which will eventually free itself by itself. This is the way in which realization develops.

Realization is Peace. As soon as we are satisfied there is peace; we can enjoy what we have. When we have loving-kindness there is peace, and when there is knowledge and wisdom, we abide in peace. If, from now onwards, we develop step by step towards the peace of realization, which transcends peace and suffering, then eventually after realization I think you will understand the Dharmakaya, the Sambhogakaya and Nirmanakaya.

The way in which Realized Beings help others does not involve effort; if there is effort then they are not Buddhas. They do it through their very nature, their essence, which is the full realization of everybody's essence and so their benefit is always there for everyone. It is not at all the sort of situation where suffering beings pray to them, they then become so deeply moved that they want to help and then they help ; never, never like that. Were it like that, all beings would have already become Buddhas, since Sakyamuni Buddha achieved enlightenment over two thousand five hundred years ago and that would have been too long a time for him to be asleep!

When our trust, devotion, diligence and moral discipline are not correct and co-ordinated, the benefit of the Buddhas or of the Transmission Lineage cannot come to us. If there is a seed then the ground must be warm and wet in order for it to grow. If it is not, how could it ever grow? A dry seed left on a table would produce nothing, even if left for ten years. Likewise a pot must be turned the right way up in order for it to hold its contents. One could pour nectar into an upturned pot for ten years and not a drop would enter. In a similar way to these examples, the teachings of the Buddha which would lead from peace to greater peace, do not work by the Buddha making effort and saying, "I want to help all beings". The teachings of the Buddha are like a lasso, not the ordinary sort of lasso with a noose that catches animals but a nooseless lassoo that one must catch and hold onto. Then it will pull one away. Or like a trap; not an ordinary trap that works by force but an open trap that one is in if one wants to be freed from suffering and the causes of suffering. But if one wants to suffer or do something else, then that trap can never trap one because it does not work by force or of its own will. It only works through the voluntary power of devotion and compassion.

When within the Madhyamaka view we speak of Dharmakaya, Sambhogakaya, Nirmanakaya and their activity, we should understand them to be free from duality. When we say that Realization is Peace, the Peace beyond peace, then the benefit of such Realization is in the path - the path which leads from peace to Peace.

## 4. All Phenomena Are Devoid of Self-Entity

This is the fourth seal. 'Self' has two main aspects: the beings' 'self' and the things' 'self'. We could say the animate self and the inanimate self. The first of these, the animate self, concerns 'I' and 'mine'.

When we say 'I', we are deluded. It is illusion. Through reason and logic this can be easily proven since for 'I' to exist it would have to have independence and be constant but since 'I' is a very dependent and relative thing, then as such it cannot have true existence. The interdependent way in which 'I' arises is just illusion and since 'I' is not here then 'mine' cannot exist either. This is all dealt with in great analytical detail in philosophy.

The no-self-entity of phenomena mainly shows the absence of self-entity (unitary, independent existence) in spacial and temporal phenomena, by analysing the smallest supposed units of substance and likewise the smallest units of time. Since there cannot be a shortest time (which would have to be an indifferentiable instant without duration), then how can there be longer true time composed of sequences of those shorter time units? If this is correct, then how did everything start and what does time mean? Similarly with particles: if the smallest particle were really the smallest then it would follow that it would be partless and directionless without inner, outer, back or front, and so on (had it these aspects then it would be divisible and hence not the smallest particle). Without such parts it can have neither dimension nor size and hence no existence. It would take a long time to expound this fully in a technically accurate way, since it comprises the whole Madhyamaka philosophy. In the Madhyamaka this understanding is developed through analysis of four main aspects: cause, result, cause and result together and the general. These analyses give rise to what are known as the *four great tenets of Madhyamaka* which are like its alphabet. Knowledge of that alphabet is the key to all Madhyamaka language.

Thus, in the ultimate truth there is no 'I' but in the relative truth 'I' exists. Because there is 'I' then the Buddha also teaches that there are no phenomena which are not interdependent. 'I' exists as a dependent phenomenon in a relative, conventional world. When 'I' create a good karmic accumulation, the good result comes to 'me', not someone else. When 'I' study it is 'I' who become well-educated. On the relative level there is nothing which is not dependent and so there is definitely an 'I'. On the ultimate level, precisely because everything is interdependent, then nothing has true existence as its essence. Everything depends upon something else and so nothing has solid independent existence. For this reason it is said that there is not anything which is permanent.

What is the outcome of all this? In one way it all seems confused yet it is not confused or confusing at all. As we train in Madhyamaka, we learn about the ultimate and relative levels of truth and how these must be understood very clearly without ever being mixed-up or confused. We are on the relative level following a path which leads to the ultimate. That ultimate is our essence, our view. The one who adopts that view and understands it is the relative person. This is why it is said in the mystical songs known as *doha*, that:

*In this universe, this world, which is illusion,*
*The illusory practitioner travels the illusory path*
*To obtain the illusory result.*

This means that according to the ultimate view, the relative is illusory, but nevertheless we who are in the illusion must try to progress, to attain realization by ridding ourselves of the obstacle of illusion. In order to eliminate these obstacles, we first have to create better illusions and remove the bad illusions.

When controlled by desire, aversion and ignorance, there is no possibility of us achieving realization. They must be removed by dropping anything which might constitute a cause or condition for their growth or development. Simultaneously, the causes of the positive must be cultivated. Thus we must stop killing and preserve life - this results in longer life. We must stop lying and tell the truth - this results in good respectable speech and environment, and so on.

All these things are positive but they are not the main thing because they are still illusion and to get rid of the illusion we must meditate, taking advantage of the good speech and healthy life to really get free from duality. An example of how this works is given by the sun, the clouds and the wind. Even when the weather is very cloudy the sun is always there. In order to remove the clouds there must be a strong wind and then the sun will be seen but still its full heat and vitality will not be felt because of the effect of the wind. The wind itself has become the obscuration and that is the next thing to be removed. We must first create a better illusion which gets rid of the worse one and then later remove the better illusion with the wisdom of non-duality.

The most important point in this brief explanation of the four seals or the four keys of Dharma is that both the relative and ultimate be included in our basic view. If one does not accept both in the basic view then it is not easy to grasp the essence of the Buddhadharma since all the teachings are based upon this twofold approach.

How can we apply this to our practice? Sometimes we are happy, sometimes unhappy. These teachings do not mean that when we feel happy we should tell ourselves, "Oh, it's nothing - just emptiness" nor does it mean that when we are miserable we should think, "Oh, it's nothing, I have to suffer". We will still suffer and be happy just like everyone else, but we should do so in the light of the understanding that happiness and suffering have no solid existence, no true existence - they are just like an illusion, an experience, a dream, and so there is no point in trying to avoid them by developing aversion towards them.

We need to try to avoid the sufferings without developing hatred towards them, without taking them for real and also to accept the happiness without making it too solid, uninvolvedly doing the best for one's family and to improve life. That is one aspect of understanding. Another aspect applies more specifically to our practice. When doing something good, practicing moral discipline and so on, we should not take our practice of virtue as something solid, or very, very special - we should just take it as it is. When doing something good, it is important to do it without a selfish motivation and without a very fixed, solid idea of good and bad. Then we can keep to the view in its entirety. Of course, we cannot manage to think like that each and every time we act, but we can accustom ourselves to this general approach.

This whole, integrated view is said to be the sign, or seal, of a true teaching of the Buddha and, as such, it is the fundamental viewpoint of Dharma.

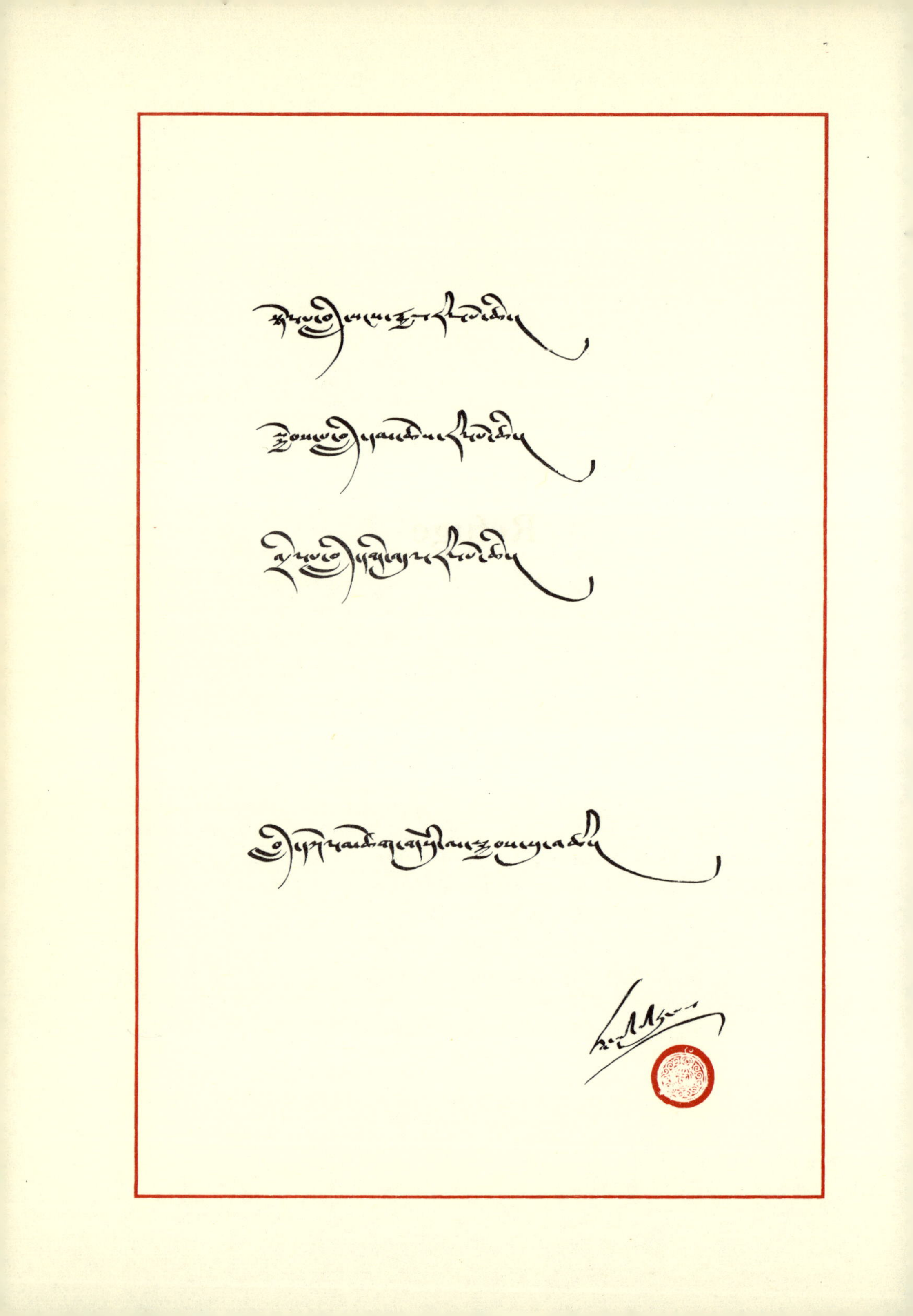

[illegible]

[illegible]

[illegible]

[illegible]

[illegible]

# Refuge

When we talk about 'refuge' it sounds as though we are taking shelter in something external but that in which we take our refuge is really something inner - the inner essence of the Buddha, Dharma and Sangha. There is an outer form of refuge wherein the Buddha is Sakyamuni, the person who achieved realization two thousand five hundred years ago, the Dharma is his teaching that we aspire to follow, and the Sangha are the masters or elders who are our guides and companions on the path.

The inner, real refuge however is the Buddha, not just the person who achieved realization but the Buddha-nature that is contained in each of us as a seed and which enables us to achieve Buddhahood just as did Sakyamuni. We say 'take refuge' or sometimes 'pay homage'; taking refuge is more than just paying homage because it means actively taking the opportunity of achieving the full liberation of what is within us, that which deserves to be manifest - the Buddha-nature.

The Dharma is the path. Even though we all want to be happy and nobody wants to suffer, nevertheless we experience so much suffering and so very little happiness. It is not because we do not want happiness that we do not get it. It is because we lack the means. Realization - the ultimate liberation - is a very difficult level of understanding to achieve without following a path and the path we need to follow is the same one that all the great masters and great beings, from the time of Buddha until the present day, have followed and through which they have all achieved their realization. Paying homage to Dharma, taking refuge in Dharma, is to make a sort of commitment to, and acknowledge our confidence in, ourselves to undertake that path.

Similarly, taking refuge in the Sangha does not only apply to the outer form - the monks, nuns and so forth. It means that we need a master or teacher to guide us as we follow the path, someone upon whom we can rely. It is, of course, possible to achieve something without a teacher but that just entails going to a bookstore, buying some Buddhist books, reading them and practicing what they teach. One can do it but one will never reap the full result since there is no transmission from the Lineage. It is the same with massage. Massage seems quite simple but if one were just to buy a book and then practice from that, it is quite possible that one could make people mad, create many diseases and so on. The beings who have already gone through the path and who have the necessary experience to guide us through it are the Sangha, and we take refuge in this Sangha as our guides and companions on the path to liberation.

In this way we take our refuge first in the outer Buddha, Sakyamuni, the outer Dharma, the teaching, and the outer Sangha which is the guidance of the masters and Bodhisattvas. Then we take refuge in the inner Buddha, the Buddha-nature, the inner Dharma, the journey of achieving realization, and the inner Sangha, acting rightly by relying upon the guidance that comes through our Lineage. These are the inner and outer forms of refuge.

Receiving the vow of refuge is not just a matter of reciting words. When it is really meant, heartfelt, then we receive not only the formal vow but the meaning of the refuge where the sense of commitment for going through with the path, and the confidence to do that, is born in us. This is the commitment to really strive for the liberation that we deserve, of which we are worthy, and we take refuge with confidence in the view by which we are now guided.

Taking the vow before a preceptor is a surer way than just taking it by ourselves. Most of the time we are too tricky and in wanting the best for ourselves we hurt ourselves. If we take the vow by ourselves we may mean it at the time but it will be much easier to become careless later. For instance, one may say, "From today onwards, I will not smoke", but then later think, "I did not really promise it to anybody in particular. It doesn't matter, it's O.K. to do it." It is a kind of trick that we use to fool ourselves. From this point of view it is important to take refuge from someone who represents the Lineage.

Just to take the vow is not enough. We have to continue to work with it on the path and so we then have to ask ourselves, "What does it mean to take refuge in the Buddha?" It means to liberate the Buddha-nature within. Because of that we cannot take refuge in anything that does not lead to that liberation. In Tibet, for example, there are many local deities: each mountain has different gods, each family has different gods and even each tree. People pay respect to them but not with the intention of taking them as a source of refuge. We just try to be friends with them and this can be done here with any gods you know - respect but not refuge. Refuge means that we take the object of our refuge as our aim and our aim is not to become a god. A god may be better than us but we do not want to become a mountain god, a lake god or a tree god. However, we need their help because the earth does not belong only to us but also to the gods and other kinds of beings too. If we do not pay respect to them then in this relative world we will get lots of trouble. It is necessary. (For example, when we build big buildings here there is no real respect for the true owners of the land - the gods. People just dig out the ground and build and the result is a lot of negativity, negative influences which cannot be seen but which can be felt. What people should do is to first request occupation from the local gods once they have decided they want to build there, almost like purchasing the land from them). The main point is that since we are taking refuge in the Buddha because we seek the great liberation, then we cannot take refuge in anything that will not bring the great liberation.

Taking refuge in the Dharma means adoption of the teachings as the path that leads to liberation. This implies that we should avoid hurting any being for selfish reasons. We make a resolution in our minds but we should be aware of the possibility of breaking that resolution. If we are sick, for instance, because of some virus or bacteria, then we may have to take medicines which will kill them and killing means even more than just hurting. We make the resolution, 'From this day forward I will never hurt any being' and we must do our best to keep that promise. Doing anything against any of the 'Three Jewels' breaks the vow and if the vow is broken then we should feel shame and guilt about what we have done; not a hopeless sense of shame or guilt but a recognition of having done something bad. We have taken refuge before our teacher, the Buddha, the Dharma and the Sangha and breaking the vow is just like trying to fool them. Guilt is the embarrassment felt before them and shame is within us even though no one else knows what we have done. Just shame and guilt would be a sort of hopeless situation. In Buddhism we use them to develop confidence in our ability never to do such things again. Knowing that something was wrong, we want to confess it and voice very strong and pure thoughts. This is the correct way to work with shame and guilt. Refuge in the Dharma, therefore, means working with the teachings.

Refuge in the Sangha means travelling with them on the path as they lead us to the right goal and this is why we should not befriend too closely 'bad' beings; those whose negativity influences us. This may sound strange but it is quite reasonable. Someone who is very involved with a life of violence, who likes stealing and killing and so on, we call a negative person. Because even such a person contains the Buddha-nature, then in the ultimate sense we cannot say that that person is negative. But relatively such a person is involved in a negative world and because of that we should not associate with them until we are strong, otherwise, instead of helping them, we will be misled and take a wrong path ourselves. Once we are strong enough we should not reject them but help them as much as we can, because our commitment is to reach liberation for the benefit of all sentient beings and those beings need more help than the good ones. So temporarily we must keep away from them and later be close to them. This is the third aspect, and these three commitments related to the three objects of refuge are the three principal refuge commitments. Then there are three more related to the representations of the Buddha, Dharma and Sangha. The Buddha is represented by statues, the Dharma by the texts and the Sangha by any image of monks, nuns, Bodhisattvas, and so forth. The way that we respect them is based upon values which are the same all over the world. Everywhere the upper half of the body is that which is respected and the lower half not so much respected. This is not just Tibetan. Because of this we do not sit on or step on the statues and the books but put them in a high place and respect them. Although Dharma people will do this there are some shops and places that use big Buddha statues as coatstands or as lampholders and this is disrespectful, like using the Buddha as a servant. The images are not to be used like that.

The essence of respect is to have a pure mind and attitude and is not in the action itself. There is an example of this. Once a person was walking along and he saw a statue of the Buddha on the ground. He thought, "If people walk over that they will create bad karma" and so he took it and placed it on the side of the street. Since his motivation was good, he created good karma. Another person came along and thought, "This Buddha statue is lying here exposed to sun and rain and will be ruined". He wanted to protect it and, looking around, he found a very old shoe which he then placed over the statue. Normally this would, of course, be a very bad thing to do but because his motivation was pure it created good karma for that person. Another person came along and saw the shoe on the Buddha and thought, "It is evil to put a shoe over the Buddha in such a way" and so he took the shoe and threw it away. That person also created good karma. Later yet another person saw the statue lying by the road and thought, "This is disrespectful and ought not to be left there",and picked up the statue and placed it on a wall, also creating good karma. It was not the actions themselves but the motivations that created the good karma. Motivation is the most important thing and respect can be shown in many ways. Respecting the images and the body, speech and mind representations of the Buddha moulds one's mind into respect. For this reason it is very important to observe the formalities of respect.

Following this there are other commitments that we subsequently develop, such as a compassionate attitude and understanding for all beings. At first we have to think, "I wish I could help others and become like medicine for others", and because of this we then really put that wish into practice and act to help others. These two aspects are known as aspiration Bodhicitta and application Bodhicitta and the vows for these are taken step by step as our commitment to help others. We are Buddhists and I became Buddhist when I was a little child. However, I am not just working for Buddhists or to make people become Buddhist; I am working for people and since Buddhism benefits people through the great wisdom of Lord Buddha's teachings then I am satisfied. We have to give up the thought, 'I want to work for Buddhism' because what we should be working for is people, through the teachings of Buddhism, and we should keep this commitment and understanding in mind. We have to be so careful to maintain awareness of the fact that we are working for beings not Buddhism. It is vitally important otherwise it all becomes a game of collecting people for Buddhism which does not mean anything. This is the basic idea of the refuge vow, its purpose and the commitments it involves.

The actual ceremony for taking the refuge vow involves repeating the refuge formula after the teacher three times. What we say, basically, is :

> *Masters, all the Buddhas and Bodhisattvas, please hear me. From now until realization, I take refuge in the Buddha, who is the example of my own nature. I take refuge in the Dharma which is the path to achieve liberation of, fulfillment of, that nature and I take refuge in the Sangha, the companions and guides on this path. All Buddhas and Bodhisattvas of the three times and the ten directions, recognize me as one who seeks refuge in the Triple Gem for the benefit of all beings.*

Because now and since beginningless time we contain the Buddha-nature, we are all in essence Buddhists. Just repeating these words cannot make us Buddhists but proper intention can. All beings, gods, animals, humans etc. have Buddha-nature in essence, on the ultimate level, and in that reality are the same as Buddhists, and when we normally say 'Buddhist', 'Christian' or 'Hindu' then these words obscure the real meaning - diminish it. Buddhists are a small group, Christians are a small group and so on. In absolute terms everybody has Buddha-nature. For instance, in the secret teachings of the Muslims (the Sufi teachings) it says that Allah is within everybody, and when they pray to Allah they are in fact praying to their Buddha-nature; it is just that the path is slightly different. When Jesus Christ picks up a little lamb and says, "I am the shepherd and all beings are like my lambs" then it is just the same as in Buddhism, where we call the greatest sort of Bodhisattva the 'one who is like a shepherd'. Shepherds look after sheep without any self-expectation: when the sheep are hungry they take them to graze, when they are thirsty they take them to the river, when it is cold they take them to the sun and when it is very hot they take them to the shade. This is how great Bodhisattvas help other beings.

In that way the real essence of Dharma always converges on one point, one meaning, which no one can ignore: the 'as-it-isness'. As one repeats the prayer of the vow one must feel that meaning. The actual receiving of the vow comes after the third repetition of the prayer when the teacher snaps his fingers. At that moment one receives the refuge from the Buddhas of the three times and the ten directions, from the Dharma, represented by the book the teacher has, and from the Sangha, represented by the ordained and non-ordained Dharma brothers and sisters present. They become our older brothers and sisters and later refuge-takers become our younger brothers and sisters. Having received the refuge vow as our formal commitment to reach the great liberation, we must maintain confidence in it. By really meaning what we say, actions will follow the words.

We say that we take refuge for the benefit of all sentient beings but at first we can only really benefit them on the relative level. Later we will be able to benefit them on the ultimate level. This comes through our realization and that realization is not something that we have to obtain or find somewhere. All we must do is purify the obscurations that we have and thus achieve the great liberation that is inherent within us. It is realization itself that holds the power to help others and our commitment to achieve it should therefore be heartfelt. We make an offering to symbolize this strong commitment, an offering of hair because the most important part of our body is our head and on the crown of the head is our hair. Offering a little of our hair to the shrine represents offering the actions, words and thoughts of our body, speech and mind to the path of liberation. Then we receive a new name, a Dharma name, to strengthen our connection with this path.

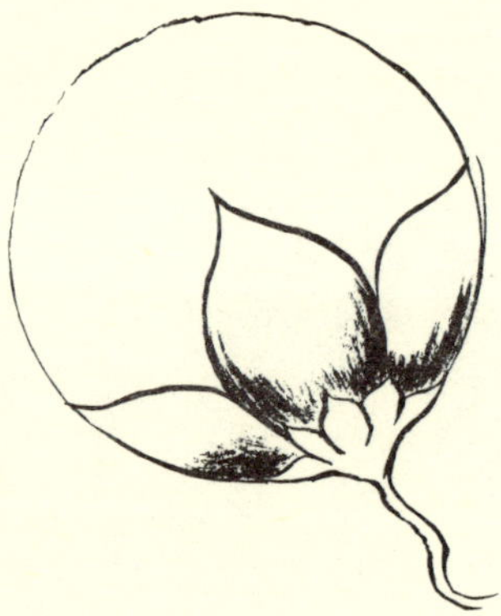

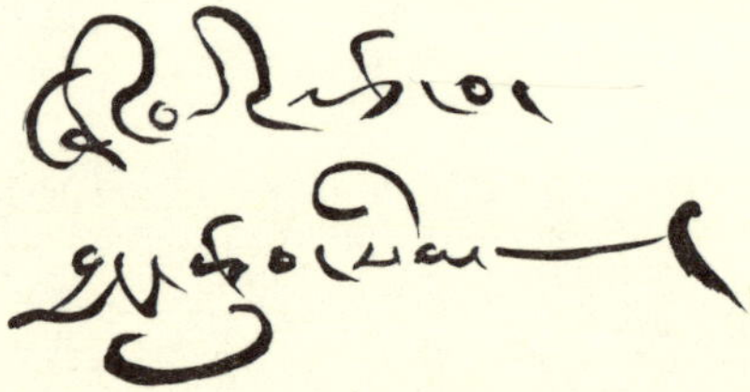

# Bodhicitta

## The Four Immeasurable Contemplations

Often when we hear about Bodhicitta we take it to mean compassion. Although this is true, there is much more to it. The Tibetan phrase for Bodhicitta is 'byan.chub.kyi.sems' which literally means 'mind of enlightenment'. This 'mind of enlightenment' is fundamental to Mahayana Buddhism since without it there can be no enlightenment. It is the beginning of all Mahayana practice. However it is not something we have to create by adopting a certain way of looking at things or understanding them. It is the seeing of everything, just as it is, by the essence of everything - the mind- without any mistake.

When considering the development of Bodhicitta we can distinguish three phases:
a) the mind of enlightenment as a basis,
b) the mind of enlightenment as a path and
c) the result, enlightenment.
The enlightened mind as a basis is the ultimate Bodhicitta, to be understood through the Madhyamaka view of non-extremity. The path - the practice of Bodhicitta - is divided into two aspects: aspiration Bodhicitta and practice Bodhicitta. The result is enlightenment - the great liberation - ultimate freedom and ultimate peace.

The great Bodhisattva Shantidéva said in the Bodhisattvacaryavatara that:

> *From the instant that Bodhicitta, the great compassion, arises, then even someone who had been formerly the most evil person in the whole universe becomes a 'son of the Buddha', the greatest of all beings.*

He is telling us that good and evil have no true existence in terms of the absolute truth; they only exist on the relative level. The essence of good and evil is not something other than that of Bodhicitta and so such change can come about if a person's motivation changes. There is a reason for saying 'Son of the Buddha': one born as a prince will grow up in his royal family and eventually become king. Once one has given rise to the Bodhicitta, the only remaining course is to develop within it and to ultimately become a Buddha.

We begin our cultivation of Bodhicitta by developing the four immeasurable contemplations. Most Tibetan prayers start with a refuge in the Buddha, Dharma and Sangha followed by these four immeasurable contemplations. The order in which these four are explained is usually different from that in which they occur in the prayer. Their order in the prayer is the following: loving- kindness, compassion, joy and impartiality. In the explanation we begin with impartiality, then come loving-kindness, compassion and joy. The actual prayer says:

May all beings have happiness and the causes of happiness,
May they all be free from suffering and the causes of suffering,
May they never be separated from the happiness which is free of all kinds of suffering and
May they abide in the great impartiality.

Impartiality is mentioned last because all the prayers that we make are for the benefit of all sentient beings, impartially, and thus it acts as the dedication. However, when we are studying, learning about the path, we must have impartiality as our basis. When we wish for beings to be happy, which beings are we talking about? All beings. For how long? Forever. Thus we begin the explanation with impartiality.

### Immeasurable Impartiality

The Buddha's teaching explains very clearly that, although this present life may have commenced a certain number of years ago, mind is beginningless. We continually take birth after birth, in samsara, for millions and billions of lives. During that time each sentient being has been our mother many times over. Even if each being had been our mother a million times this would be a small figure compared to the total number of births. This is why the object of our practice is to help all of these mother beings equally. They are all in need of help, just as are we.

Although nothing has true existence, we tend to take everything as real, and we waste a lot of time being under the control of that 'reality's' illusion. Just as we do not want to suffer through this illusion, neither does any other being and so we should wish to help them all equally. In this particular relative world we feel close to those dear or related to us and distant from strangers, but in the ultimate truth these feelings are invalid. Once we think about it, friendship and enmity in this life make little sense. We often see people who were once great friends and who are now our enemies. Likewise people who were once enemies are friends. The situation of one moment never stays frozen, the same. Each day, each minute, each second it changes and because the notions of friend and enemy are just illusory ideas, they also change. If they were not illusory they would not be changeable.

There is an historical example which shows the fragility of friendship. The great master Katyayana was a Hinayana practitioner who achieved freedom. From time to time he could see the past and the future. One day he was walking through the street to beg his food when he saw a person sitting on a seat eating a fish. The person threw a fish bone to the ground and a dog came and started eating it. The person kicked the dog angrily. As Katyayana watched this he perceived that the fish was the reincarnation of that person's late father and that the dog was the reincarnation of the late mother. Katyayana was amazed at how karma worked and at the illusory nature of the world. There is nothing real in it. That person was sitting comfortably in a chair eating the flesh of his father and kicking his mother!

Any prayer we make or positive accumulation should be done with the attitude that it may be for the benefit of all beings. This is what is meant by immeasurable impartiality, otherwise we might understand that term to mean a sort of neutrality, or something empty. If it were like that it would not mean anything. Impartiality means that we are inviting all beings to be our guests and share the relative and ultimate benefits of our practice. As Shantidéva says:

*Today I invite all beings to be my guests,*
*To share the happiness of the moment and of ultimate peace.*
*Before all the Buddhas and Bodhisattvas*
*Whose wisdom-eyes see the whole circle of time,*
*I pray that all beings, from gods to hell-beings,*
*May enjoy my offering of relative and ultimate happiness.*

### Immeasurable Loving-Kindness

The second of the four immeasurable contemplations is loving-kindness. Put briefly, this is the wish that all beings may have happiness and the causes of happiness. Why? Among all our mother sentient beings there is not one that does not want to be happy. Even those who cause themselves suffering do so from the wish for happiness, not seeing that what they are doing is in fact the cause of suffering and thus mistakenly accumulating great misery instead of great happiness. What is wished for, in that case, and what is obtained are totally opposite. This is the suffering of samsara. Every sentient being has formerly been as kind to us as a mother is to her only child and so now we accept the responsability to be a kind mother to beings, as if each were our only child. Even in the most ignorant realm there is not a mother who does not want the best for her child, but often she will cause more harm than good because her loving efforts are guided by ignorance. Until now we have been like this. Now things are different. We have discovered the path of loving-kindness based upon great understanding, as taught by the Buddha; the eighty-four thousand methods to enlightenment. Without feeling too proud of ourselves, we can confidently develop this loving-kindness towards all our mother sentient beings until we reach the point where we consider them more important than ourselves. This love is to be cultivated without any expectation of return; we should be like a mother bird caring for her egg. The egg has no claws or beak with which to protect itself - it is totally powerless. Even though she could just fly away at any time, the mother bird sits on it, warms it patiently and guards it until it hatches and opens to its new world. She does all that through her natural loving-kindness, acting without fear of failure or hope of reward. This is how our loving-kindness towards all sentient beings should be.

## Immeasurable Compassion

The third of the four immeasurable contemplations is that of compassion. Compassion is the wish that all beings may be free from suffering and its causes. No being wants to suffer - even for a moment. The problem is that they just do not know how to avoid suffering.

At present, all that we know about things is their apparent nature. We know that if we put our hand in the fire it will get burnt. It is not just the fire's fault; it is the combined fault of the fire and our ignorance. Through the ignorance of dualistic thinking, the fire and our body have become separate. Because of the dualistic split anything can be the cause of suffering and quite often beings will create the cause of an intense future suffering when they are just trying to avoid a slight suffering (for example, creating the strong karma of killing animals to remove the slight suffering of hunger). In this way the causes of suffering are being constantly created. How then can we know the right way to act? It is very simple. We put ourselves in the place of others, and others in our place, then it is very easy to see, on the relative level, what to do. Through a gradual development of such awareness, further levels of understanding will emerge.

In the Prajnaparamita Sutra, the Buddha gives seventeen groups of teaching devoted solely to the explanation of voidness. The largest of these teachings is in a twelve volume work which covers all seventeen groups. In this work, called the "Summary of all Dharma", the Buddha says,

*"He who wishes to realize Buddhahood,*
*The Ultimate Truth just as it is,*
*Should not practice many things,*
*But one thing - immeasurable great Compassion."*

Asanga was one of the greatest Buddhist masters and one of the six (sometimes eight)'Ornaments of our World'. He received the Five Teachings of Maitreya from Maitreya himself. Before entering Tushita, the pure dimension of Maitreya, he had meditated on Maitreya for twelve years but in those twelve years he achieved no tangible result from his practice. Why? Because his compassion was not great enough. However, during the twelve years he did manage to remove some obscurations and gather some understanding and wholesomeness. Shortly after his twelve years of retreat, he was passing through a narrow ravine when he heard a dog bark. Looking around he saw a dog, the lower part of whose body was completely worm-infested and rotten. The upper part of its body was healthy and it was barking at him angrily. His compassion welled up and he thought: "This miserable dog is full of suffering and without strength but it still has attachment to its body and hatred for me because I am a strong and healthy human. What ignorance! I myself and all beings are controlled in this way by ignorance".

Without feeling pity for the dog, he developed very pure compassion. He thought, "If I leave now the dog will die but if I stay and remove the worms, they will die". He thought and thought until he concluded that the only way the worms could survive would be for them to have fresh flesh and that the only way the dog could survive was by having all the worms removed. Perceiving his own body as a heap of flesh, he cut a large piece from his upper leg and placed it on one side. His first thought was to remove the worms with a twig, but he soon realized that this would inevitably harm some of them. He even thought of using his fingers but they too were not delicate enough. Then he realized that the softest part of his body was his tongue and so he closed his eyes and leant forward to take off the first worms. He lowered his head expecting to feel the worms but it eventually touched the ground and so he opened his eyes. The dog was no longer there. Looking up he saw Maitreya Buddha before him.

Until that moment his compassion had been too feeble but in that moment his compassion was pure. His twelve years of hard, solitary practice in the cave was exceeded a billionfold by the power of that moment's pure compassion for the miserable dog. In fact, he said to Maitreya,

> *I have been practicing for so long without result, why did you not appear before?*

Maitreya Buddha answered:

> *Since your first session of meditation I was with you but you had no compassion and expected too much. That is why you could not see me. If you do not believe me I will come onto your shoulder by using my spiritual power. Just walk through the streets and observe what people see.*

Asanga walked through the streets awaiting the people's reactions. Nobody seemed to see anything at first and the only people to see something at all were a porter, who thought he was carrying a little dog on his shoulder, and a woman wine-seller, who saw a big foot on his shoulder. Then Asanga really believed and he subsequently received the Five Great Shastras from Maitreya, just as we know them now. This is a genuine story. It really happened that way and this story shows us, proves to us, how love and compassion are the most important things.

Compassion has many aspects and in the Mahayana it is taught as living compassion and skilful means. All the ways of being compassionate are wonderful, of course, but without right method they cannot help others properly. A mother may have great compassion for her only child but if she has no hands and the child falls into the river then she will be helpless, all she can do is scream and shout. Even though she has so much love she can do nothing for her child. Therefore since only a limited benefit can emerge from lifeless, blind love or compassion, the Dharma teachings show us how to practice compassion which is alive and skilful and this is why it is called the immeasurable great compassion.

## Immeasurable Great Joy

The fourth of the four immeasurable contemplations is great joy. This is the opposite of regret and jealousy - a rejoicing in the goodness of others and their positive qualities. Normally jealousy and resentment are focused on the relative happiness of beings but that relative happiness is just like a feast in a dream. If as Mahayana Buddhists we are jealous, then what we propound and what we do are completely contradictory, since we are trying to accumulate what is positive and to not be trapped by the illusion. Whatever kind of happiness others enjoy and whatever causes or conditions of happiness they create, we *must* rejoice in it, feel happy about it and all of our happiness must be dedicated to others. Why? Because our attitude and motivation are critically important. Buddha teaches that virtue and non-virtue, good or bad, depend only upon the way of thinking, not upon apparent nature. The meaning of what we say depends on what we mean and not upon what we say. For Buddhists, right motivation, right view, and right thinking are very important. If our thought and motivation are pure then our path and achievement will be pure. If our thought and motivation are impure then our path and achievement will also be impure.

At the time of Milarépa there was a monk named Geshe Ben. Whilst Milarépa was a hermit living in caves and caring nothing for his appearance, Geshe Ben was an esteemed monk living in a monastery. One day one of his disciples, a sponsor who was rich and important, was coming to visit Geshe Ben and so he made a very special shrine, cleaning all the statues and offering-bowls. Just before the sponsor arrived, Ben thought, "Why am I now making this shrine so nice when for such a long time I have given it no special attention?" He concluded that it could only be because the person who was coming was important to him. He rushed to the kitchen, took a handful of ashes, returned to the shrine and scattered them all over, making it very dirty. The disciple arrived - everything was a mess. Some time later, Milarépa heard of this story and said:

In all of Tibet there has been no finer offering
Than the offering of ashes of the monk Ben.

This does not mean that we should dirty our shrines; it means that our intention is most important.

There is another story about a master who could perceive the rebirths taken by beings; he could also read their thoughts. Below his cave there ran a mighty river and one day a mother and her daughter were attempting to cross it. Unfortunately, they were both swept away by the strength of the current. As she was being carried off, the mother thought, "Now I am done for but I do not care as long as my daughter is safe." The daughter was thinking, "Now I am done for but it does not matter as long as my mother is safe." They both died. Because of their pure motivation, their loving-kindness, which although relative was nevertheless pure, both were reborn in the realm of the gods. All our practice, everything we do, depends upon our motivation. When it is pure then what we do is pure; when it is impure then what we accomplish is impure.

There is another story concerning negative thoughts. There was once a beggar at the gate of the palace of a certain king. The beggar thought, "If the king were to die tomorrow morning through someone cutting his throat, it is possible that I might become king in his place." He thought that really strongly - he meant it. The next morning one of the king's guards rode his chariot out of the palace gate and the chariot wheel ran over the neck of the sleeping beggar, cutting off his head. All that we experience is the result of what we accumulate. What we accumulate may be good, bad or neutral and the goodness, badness or neutrality depends entirely upon what we mean and not upon the actions themselves.

Why are the four contemplations called immeasurable? Because they have no limit and because they transcend time. When, for example, we say, "May all beings have happiness and the causes of happiness" we do not mean that to apply to a certain group of beings, wishing them a specific sort of happiness for a limited duration of time. We mean limitless beings to have every sort of happiness forever.

There are many ways of practicing Bodhicitta, suitable for beings at different levels of spiritual development. We are all on different levels, some having more 'outer' knowledge and with a great external activity and some with very deep understanding. However, there is a basic practice which is suitable for everyone because it is so simple. Being simple, it is deep and beneficial; beneficial because its simplicity means there will be few mistakes. We begin with loving-kindness, working at the level of our present understanding and with our present conception of the world, by trying to imagine the nicest, purest form of happiness we know. This will vary from person to person but it does not matter - we just think of the very best thing and as soon as we have formed it in the imagination we share it with all beings, praying that they may have this happiness equally. Not to think of ourselves but just about others, wishing them this relative happiness we think so nice, is the first step. It makes little sense in the ultimate but it is, on our level, a start.

The next step is to call to mind any friend or acquaintance who is happier or better off than we are and just to try to be happy for them, appreciate their achievement. We think of friends first because it is easier. We meditate in this way until we really mean it and have heartfelt appreciation. Then we do the same, but for someone who is not so close to us. When we can do this we move on to someone who is not very kind to us and try to appreciate, pray for, their happiness. Then we progress to someone who is really cruel to us, who really hates us and finally to someone that we really hate. If they hate us, it is minor; if we hate them it is major because our hatred makes practice very hard - there are many strong feelings to overcome.

These exercises concern happiness and working with what we conceive to be good. We can apply the same to the negative. First we have to think of the bad things, the suffering, the things we absolutely do not want. Having imagined it, we think of taking this suffering from the person we hold most dear - our mother, father, brother, sister, friend - it could be anyone but it is certain that our mother and father are most important. Then, as before, we extend the meditation step by step, through acquaintances, strangers, enemies etc. until we are truly able to take their suffering.

Thus we develop the relative aspect of Bodhicitta but we should not take the happiness and suffering that we give and take as being real things. They are not solid. There is one way of applying this practice where the suffering taken is visualized as black smoke and the happiness given visualized as fresh and nice in colour. This practice is very suitable for certain levels of practitioner but it is not necessary to think in terms of dirtiness and cleanliness and so forth; just about goodness and badness. What we want, they also want; what we do not want, they also do not want and so we just give all that is good to others and take all the badness to ourselves.

This sort of relative attitude is just the starting point: all the nine yanas start there. When they are understood properly, the four immeasurable contemplations are the qualities of the enlightened mind. The ultimate aspect of Bodhicitta is that goodness and badness have no true existence - they are like a good dream and a nightmare. Both are impermanent and as we understand them more and more deeply, we see they have no essence, no heart, no true existence.

## The Bodhisattva's Commitments

*The commitments, vows, that the Bodhisattva undertakes, show him what he should, and what he should not, do. These are in two main parts: the Vows of aspiration and the Vows of Practice.*

### THE VOWS OF ASPIRATION

These can be gathered into five main points, the first of which is that *we should never abandon any being* since this would break our Bodhicitta commitment. To abandon someone means not to be willing to help him under any circumstance. We may not be able to help some beings now but we can keep them in mind and aspire to help them later.

The second is *always to call to mind the relative and ultimate benefits of Bodhicitta* so as not to lose its full power. It is very easy to understand. Let us take the example of, say, two people of the same age and similar situation who have incurable cancer: one understands Dharma and so knows that what is happening to him is due to a karmic cause and not just an immediate physical cause; the other believes that it is just happening now and has no understanding of karma. He will suffer because he thinks, "I wanted so much to be happy like my friends, but I can only lie here. Why should this happen to me?" and the more he thinks like this the more unbearable it will become. The person who understands Dharma knows that he has the karmic potential for such suffering and that it is ripening. He understands why such a thing should happen to him even if he does not know all the details precisely. If his understanding is a little deeper than that, he will know that his karmic experience is like the broom that clears away the causes of suffering.

When suffering appears in our life, its cause is finally no longer there and, in this way, any suffering we undergo is purifying our karma. This does not mean that we *have* to suffer, but if we do it is because we have made some mistake in a former life. The example was to show that in negative circumstances we should always keep our awareness of Bodhicitta, applying all that we know of it to our life-situation.

Similarly, on the positive side, let us imagine two businessmen, equally successful. The one with Dharma understanding knows that if he is enjoying success then it must be because of former good action. He will pursue his success and turn its benefits to other people's welfare and to creating future good. The other person, who lacks such understanding, just thinks that he is successful because he is better than others. This only reinforces his ego and hurts him instead of benefitting him. The amount of benefit that one generates depends upon one's understanding of karma. We should remember this all the time and keep working with it.

The third point is to *accumulate wisdom and merit* thereby strengthening the Bodhicitta. The accumulation of merit or virtue, is likened to making the right container and the development of wisdom is the nectar it can contain. The fourth point is to *practice the source, the main body and the action of Bodhicitta* - this increases the Bodhicitta. Practicing the source means meditating upon the four immeasurable contemplations. The main body of Bodhicitta is the refuge wish to enter Bodhicitta. The action is the dedication to all beings of all the positive or favourable things that happen to us: wealth, fame, happiness, good health, wisdom and so forth. Undedicated virtue is like an unplanted seed that can never develop. Dedicated virtue (that is, virtue that we dedicate to the benefit of all beings) is like a seed that has been planted in the ground; it will ripen producing maybe fifty similar seeds, which in their turn will make several hundred and then several thousand and so on. Therefore the action, that of dedicating virtue, is like cultivating that virtue so that it grows and flourishes.

The fifth point is to *abandon the four dark dharmas and to practice the four light ones:* this makes our Bodhicitta continue forever. If the four dark dharmas, or actions, are explained first then it is easy to understand the four light ones.

* The first dark dharma is to cheat those worthy of respect or, as we sometimes say, 'worthy of offerings'. This means to deceive the Triple Gem (the Buddha, the Dharma and the Sangha), or the Three Roots (the Guru who is the root of blessing, the Yidam who are the root of accomplishment and the Protectors who are the root of activity), or our mother, father or teachers - to deceive them through some selfish motivation.

* The second dark dharma is to cause someone to regret what should not

be regretted. If, say, someone were to give up ordinary things in order to meditate or practice some other virtue, doing so with a very pure motivation, and we were to say to that person, "You are stupid! Why are you doing that? It is meaningless to give up your things like that and bother trying to help others",then we will make that person feel bad when he is doing something that is right. We are creating regret for what should not be regretted.

* The third dark dharma is to criticize the Three Jewels or the Three Roots thinking our own judgment best. For example we could say, "Milarépa had no education and could not get a job in ordinary life - that is why he ran off to the mountains and stayed in a cave." We should avoid this sort of comparison.

* The fourth dark dharma is to cheat any being for selfish benefit.

The four light actions are the opposite of the above. If we can keep all these five points then we are maintaining our aspiration Bodhicitta.

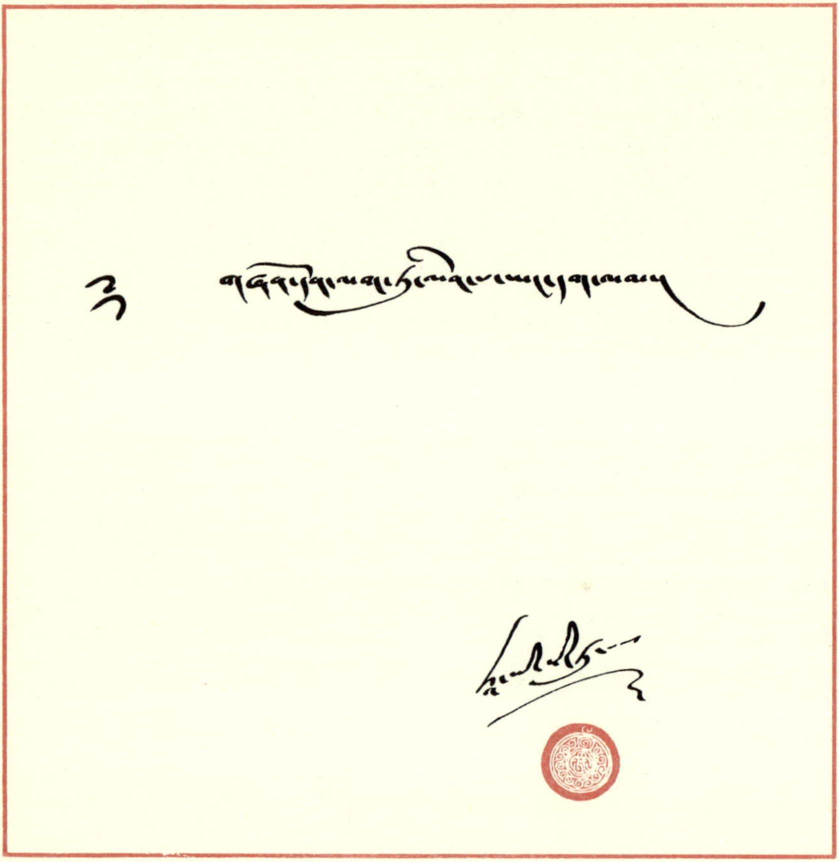

## THE VOWS OF PRACTICE BODHICITTA - The Six Paramitas

Aspiration Bodhicitta is the basis for the Bodhisattva's actual practice. All aspects of this practice are covered by the 6 paramitas and the term 'paramita' (para = other, mita = shore Skt) covers the development aspect (that which will carry one to the other shore) and the fully-developed aspect of the other shore (the perfect practice of the enlightened ones, sometimes called the 'perfections'). The 6 paramitas are generosity, skilful conduct, forbearance, diligence, meditation, and prajna (deep understanding).

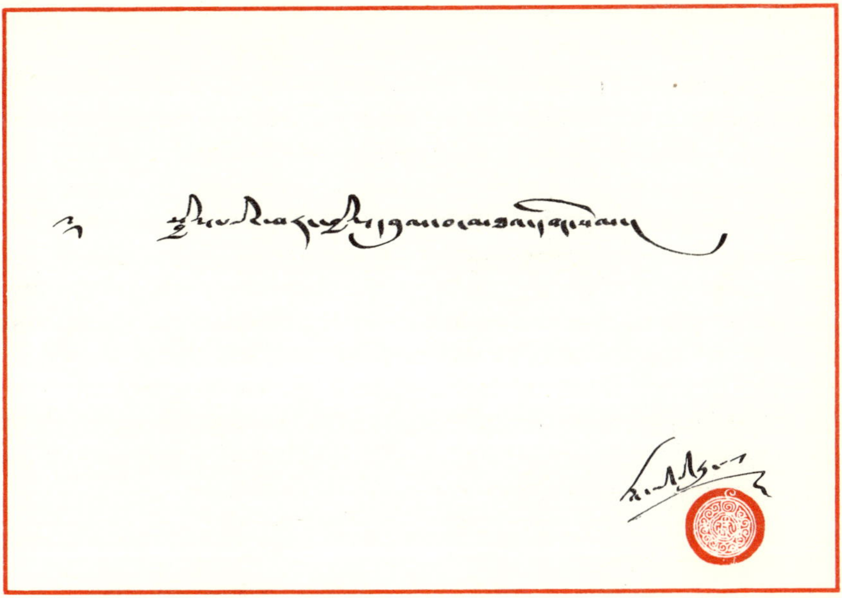

### *Generosity*

The practice of generosity is to give what is worthwhile and to give it with non-attachment. This can be studied through three main aspects: giving things, giving loving protection and giving loving understanding. The teaching on the first of these, *material generosity*, explains what is proper generosity and what is improper. We should abandon improper generosity and practice the proper one.

Motivation is very important when we give. If we give with a wrong motivation, such as making gifts which we hope will harm others or which we intend to bring us fame, or if we give with an inferior motivation such as through fear of future poverty, then that is improper. What we actually give is also important. A Bodhisattva should never give what is harmful, for instance, when he gives something suitable it should be generously, not meanly.To whom we give to is important - always pandering to the wishes of the crazy and the gluttonous would not be proper generosity. Finally, how we make our gift is important. The Bodhisattva avoids reluctant giving, angry giving, disrespectful giving and scornful, derisory giving, all of which are improper.

Proper generosity is to give whatever we have and there are many wonderful, inspiring stories of great Bodhisattvas who have given their own flesh to nourish starving animals. Whatever we can manage to give, we give to those who need it, paying particular attention to help those who represent the Three Jewels, those who have helped us - our parents especially - whose who are sick and unprotected, and also those who are our particular enemies or rivals. The way in which we make our gift to them should be joyfully, respectfully, with a compassionate heart and without regret. It is better to give with one's own hand rather than through others, to give at just the right time, and, of course, to give without harming others. Impartial giving is best and a wise person gives just what is needed.

The second form of generosity is to *give our loving protection* to those in fear: in fear of others, in fear of sickness and death and in fear of catastrophe. The third form of generosity is to make the *priceless gift of Dharma.* This does not mean indiscriminately preaching to anyone and everyone. It means helping those who have respect for the Dharma, for the truth, to understand it. With a very pure motivation, we should humbly and compassionately pass on the authentic teachings that we ourselves have understood well from a proper teacher. The thing to avoid is a mixture of personal opinion and the classical teachings and, of course, any sort of self-centred motivation. The truth is something both rare and precious and deserves to be talked about in a pleasant way and in a proper place. The classical way to give teachings is well discussed in the Sutras and, in a general way, we should know better than to jumble Dharma with worldly conversation.

These are the three basic forms of generosity. It was the first of the paramitas to be taught by the Buddha because it is one of the easiest to understand and everyone can practice it. It is also the foundation for the other five paramitas.

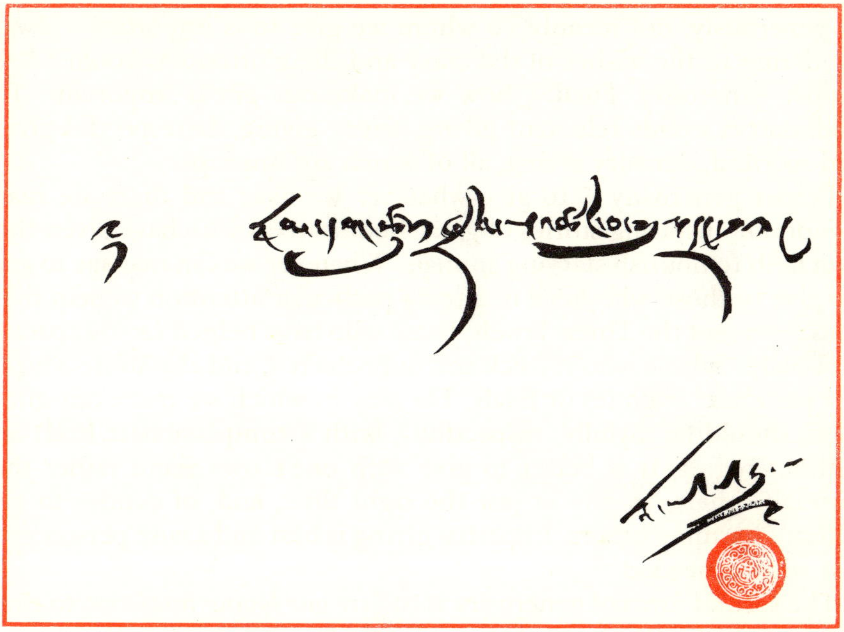

### *Skilful Conduct*

This also has three main aspects: to refrain from negative actions, to accumulate what is positive and to help others. *To refrain from negative actions* means not to do that which hurts others and that which is selfish. In general, the harmful things are those discussed under the ten non-virtues: killing, stealing, sexual misconduct, lying, slander, harsh speech, useless speech, covetousness, ill-will and misguided belief. However, if the motivation is pure then the first seven (the non-mental ones) are permissible. Since motivation is the critical factor and is mental then obviously the last three non-virtues can never be permissible. If motivation is impure then one can never be a pure Bodhisattva. To be pure, skilful, moral or proper in our conduct then we must study and learn which things are negative by training under the guidance of someone who really knows what they are and who has experience of their significance.

From amongst all the negative things we discover, we then select those we are certain of avoiding and undertake vows or commitments concerning them. For example, if we are able to stop killing then we take a vow never to kill. If we can avoid killing and stealing then we take a vow never to do either. Having made commitments never to do those of the non-virtues about which we have confidence, we set about reducing our weaknesses regarding the others and gradually try to achieve freedom from them all.

The second aspect, *accumulation of what is positive,* can be applied to anything. It is said in the Buddhist teaching that there is nothing which could not be the Bodhisattva's practice. There can be as many practices as there are phenomena and any of these, positive or negative, could present an opportunity which the Bodhisattva could turn into benefit for beings. Whatever is beneficial should be practiced according to the guidelines of the 6 paramitas. To enact these positive accumulations there must be a readiness to act - this readiness is in itself a positive accumulation.

The Mahayana methods are very simple and very skilful. If, for example, we have desire then it may not be necessary to have to exert a great effort in order to stop it. First we understand it, then we develop an understanding, an appreciation, of contentment. Decrease of desire and increase of satisfaction will occur simultaneously with our understanding of satisfaction. The one effort of understanding acts on all three fronts at once - there is no need to work on decreasing desire, increasing satisfaction and developing understanding separately. In this way all kinds of skilful wisdom can be developed and put into practice: diligence is the antidote for laziness, wisdom is the antidote for ignorance, meditation is the antidote for mental complexity, generosity is the antidote for meanness and so on. Mahayana Buddhism explains all these practices and one starts by applying the easiest for oneself and develops until one can do all that needs to be done.

The third aspect of skilful action is to *benefit others.* To really benefit them purely and properly, we have to achieve a certain level of realization so that our altruistic activity is never mistaken. We can, however, begin to benefit others even if we do not have such realization as long as we have the full conviction of pure motivation. Then we follow four basic guidelines:

* To provide others with whatever they need, to help them and to fulfil their wishes, provided that what we do will not harm them or others.
* To say that which others expect to hear according to their wishes, provided that what we say does not harm them. This means to speak nicely, not harshly, but if it is necessary to use hard words for their benefit and we are certain that this will be useful then we have to use them.
* If we can in any way give others a glimpse of the truth, even the smallest glimpse, then we must do it.
* Regardless of the level of our spiritual development and no matter whether we actually need to or not, we should act in accordance with accepted norms and customs.

Ultimately our ability to help others is limited until we have understanding and wisdom (and confidence in these). It is also limited until we reach the point where we are sure that our activity, whatever the situation, will not be impaired by disappointment or obscured by pride. Nevertheless, we start from whatever level we have obtained and help others in whatever limited way we can, according to our understanding.

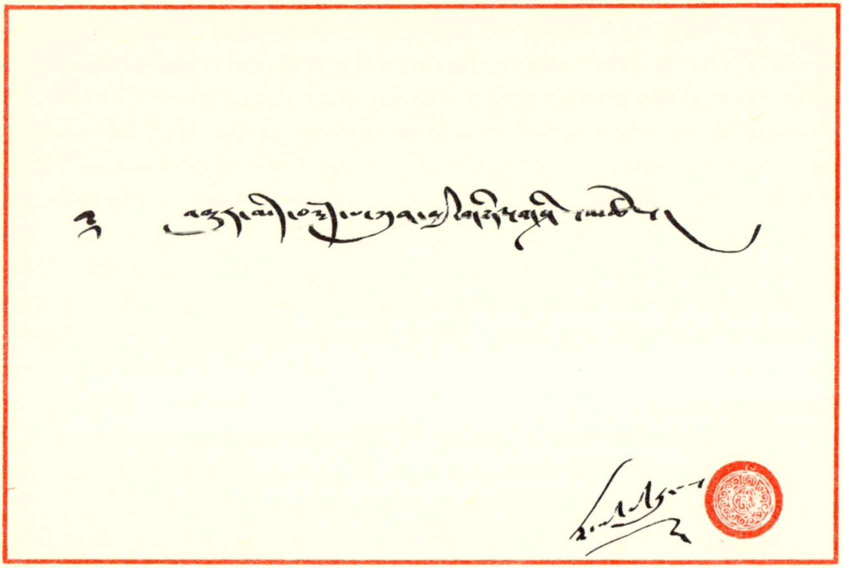

***Forbearance***

This too can be explained through three principal aspects. The first is to refrain from hurting those who have hurt us. The second is to cope with whatever suffering we have to endure, without fighting it uselessly or developing strong feelings of resentment. The third is to have confidence in the ultimate truth.

*Non-retaliation* means that when someone hits us, abuses us, does anything to injure us, our possessions or those dear to us, or anything which might increase our anger, we do not react negatively. Very simply, it means that when we are struck, if we hit that person in return then they have really struck us; if we do not retaliate, they have not really struck us. Furthermore, it is not that their blow came from nowhere. It arose from causes and conditions created in the past; it is the result of some cause that we ourselves have generated. By just accepting that blow, the cause of that particular suffering is removed, and at the same time the blow itself can become the object of diligent practice. Thus the striking becomes beneficial rather than harmful.

This is a very easy thing to say but very hard to practice. This was especially true in Tibet where, through the cultural conditioning which totally ignored the proper way of dealing with the situation, anyone who did not retaliate when struck was looked down upon; they felt ashamed. I saw, though, something which really amazed me when I was in Sikkim. There was a monk there who was a very nice and very funny man. One day he made a frivolous comment to another monk who was short-tempered. This other monk was angered by his remarks and first kicked him and then struck him on the head with a piece of wood. The monk who had been struck remained as soft as cotton, without getting uptight or angry and said, "Thank you, thank you very much. If there was no one with anger, I would never be able to develop my forbearance. Thank you." He really meant what he was saying. When such a situation arises we have to be ready to cope with it in that way. We have to begin with the most simple things: first, when someone says something annoying but not very important then we just say, "Yes, yes - it's very true." We do not really mean that but it saves argument and we must avoid being led into argument. What they say is just words. By developing forbearance on the less relevant things, we will eventually be able to deal with the difficult ones.

The second aspect of forbearance concerns *not avoiding suffering.* It does not mean that we should look for suffering or be happy to suffer, even if it does sound like that. From beginningless time until the present, each individual being has been suffering in the six realms of existence. During that enormous span of time it is certain that we have suffered billions of centuries in the hell realms, billions of centuries in the animal realm and so forth. In one way, it could be said that all that suffering was beneficial because we are here at present and have little suffering. In another way, it has not really done much good. Now as we sit down to a session of meditation, we have very little forbearance or patience, and it is a great effort to sit in the right posture, form the right attitude of mind and recite the necessary things. If we do have the forbearance, it will be highly beneficial for both ourselves and others. Buddha practiced intensively for six years on the banks of the river Neranjara before achieving his enlightenment at Bodh Gaya. The result of his endeavour has endured until the present day and will continue until the end of everything. That benefit was not only for this planet but for all beings in all states. Thus, we should not regard as difficulties all our petty troubles encountered in meditation and Dharma practice.

Sometimes we do suffer intensely, when we are sick and so on. When we are sick we should resort to medicines and when we get into trouble with people we should try to get out of that trouble. Definitely. However, our attitude to the suffering and the trouble should not be one that defines them as solely negative. Suffering is like a broom that sweeps away the causes of suffering and when we understand this then the suffering is reduced to its true stature. Without the understanding it tends to become amplified to twice, ten or a hundred times its true size. The way we develop our understanding is to think, "The suffering that I am now experiencing is the result of previous karmic causes. Just as I do not want to suffer, neither does any being. Thus may this present suffering be of true benefit in removing the sufferings of all beings." In such a way we mentally take the sufferings of all beings to ourselves and remove them by our own suffering.

If we do not do this with the fullest confidence and if there is no karmic connection between ourselves and those suffering whereby their suffering can be removed by us, then this practice can only benefit our Mind Training and cannot actually help them. If we really mean what we think then it can accomplish much more than just the taking of their suffering to ourselves. Practice involving such thinking is called tong.len in Tibetan: taking (len) the sufferings of others and giving (tong) them our happiness.

The third sort of forbearance is *to have confidence in the excellent qualities of the Three Jewels.* It comes about through taking refuge in the Buddha, Dharma and Sangha and through practicing Dharma. We should constantly remember to seek our inspiration in the Three Jewels and to apply ourselves to comprehending the absolute and relative aspects of truth. In the relative world, karma, cause and effect, exist and we should do good and avoid bad action. In the absolute truth there is neither good nor bad and all is seen as illusion. To strive hard to understand these two simultaneous levels of truth, hard for most people to grasp, especially to understand the absolute, is to forbear the ultimate truth.

We start the practice of this third aspect from a very basic position, such as the understanding of the precious human existence, how good our life is and how we can do whatever we wish with it. We have exactly what is right for us to be good - all the required qualities are present in this precious human body. Since we have these qualities it would be a waste not to use them. If a poor family has a hundred kilos of gold buried beneath the floor of their house and yet do not dig it up to use it to buy food and so forth, then they are wasting the gold's value;it servesfor nothing. In exactly the same way is our human life of great value ; it is extremely precious but if we do not use it, it is just wasted. It will not last very long. By developing such understanding to the point where we use our lives to the full, and then deepening the understanding step by step, we cultivate this third aspect of forbearance.

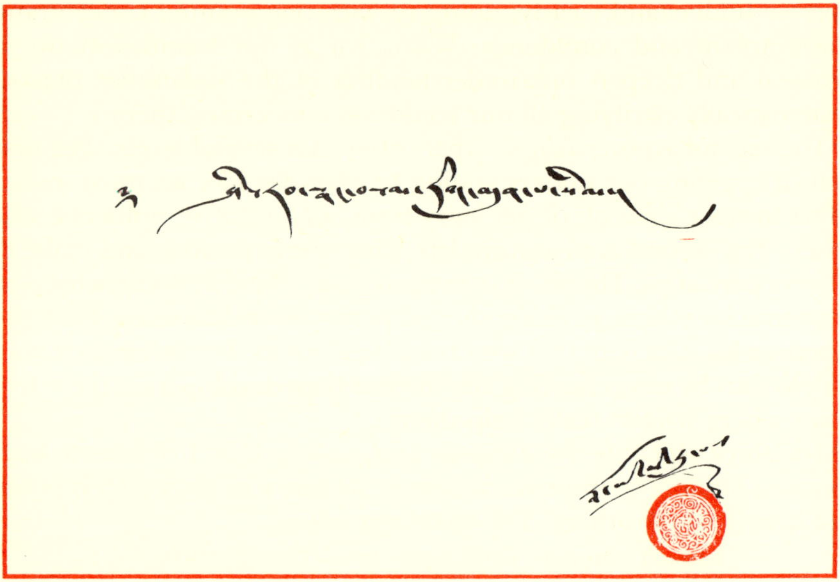

## *Diligence*

The three aspects of diligence are

* the armour-like diligence,
* the diligence of working with effort, applying our knowledge to our way of life and
* the diligence of never being satiated with our accumulation of the positive.

The first of these, the *armour-like diligence,* is based upon the thought or commitment, 'From this very moment on, I will use this precious human existence to attain realization of the ultimate truth for the sake of all beings, so that I may lead them away from suffering and all its causes.' That heartfelt thought is the beginning of the armour-like diligence. Just as armour protects us from the sharpness of weapons, diligence protects us from the power of laziness in all its forms. Otherwise laziness will pull us back, diminish our effort. First we have to learn what we should be doing and then we need to apply ourselves to the practices that we understand clearly, doing so with one-pointed concentration, commitment and confidence. With that as our foundation, we can broaden and deepen our understanding of the unfamiliar practices, systematically clarifying all our confusion concerning them.

The second aspect, *diligent application,* has several levels. The first is that in applying our understanding to everyday life, we must make an effort to steer clear of, or get away from, any negative influence which arises. The second is to accumulate whatever is positive and make that a living part of us. The third is to exert great effort in doing whatever is beneficial for others, in either the temporary or eternal sense. In all these practices we start with that which is easiest for us. For instance, it is very easy to start by never hurting anyone and then develop from there to the point where we can really help them.

The third aspect is the *diligence of dissatisfaction.* It means to have a constant longing to improve whatever we know or do which is positive and beneficial for others. The teachings tell us:

*Even if you are going to die tomorrow morning,*
*Still you should learn more,*
*Even if you have helped everybody,*
*Still you should help them once more.*

If we consider friends and enemies, then to have one billion friends would not be enough and to have even one enemy would be to have too many. We should never be satisfied with our positive accumulations, always recommencing our practice from the very beginning, from the tiniest, simplest things. Whenever we see something which could be done to bring benefit for others, no matter how small, then we should do it, take hold of the opportunity. Whatever is harmful to others we must take any opportunity to stop. Just to avoid the issue and think it does not matter is not good enough. Say, for example, we see a piece of broken glass lying on the ground. It is so simple and easy; we just pick it up and put it in a waste bin. What we do not do is to think, "Oh, there are thousands of people who pass by here - none of them has picked it up so why should I?" Each of us has equal responsibilities. If we consider one drop as nothing, then the ocean is nothing because it is composed of drops. If, however, we can accumulate the individual drops one by one, this may one day make a whole ocean.

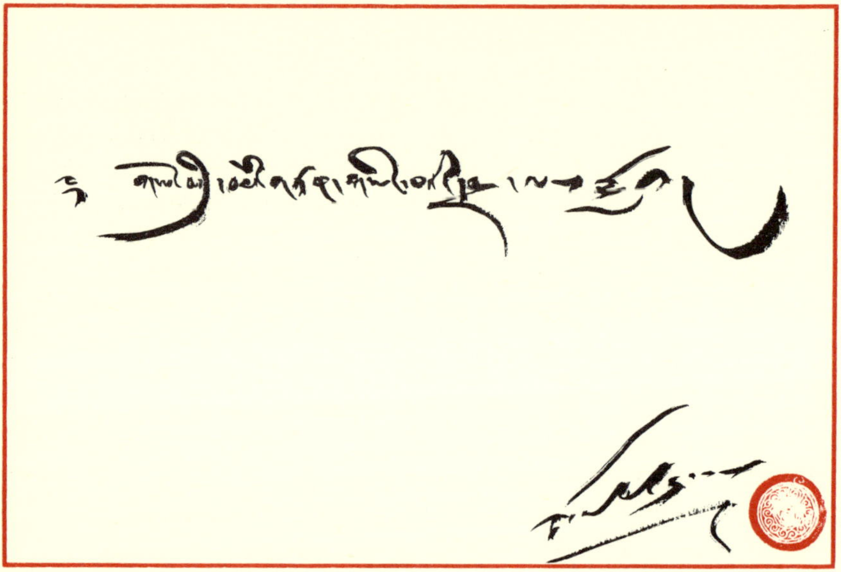

### *Meditation*

The first aspect of meditation is the *development of an inner awareness* that acquaints one with the mind as it really is, beneath its superficial layer of obscuration. When there is no practice of meditation it is impossible to practice generosity, skilful conduct, forbearance and diligence fully - they cannot become 'perfections' because their very essence, this inner awareness is lacking. In order to get to know our mind as it is, we first practice samatta (Tib.shi-nay) meditation. This makes the mind more tranquil and lets it rest in its own qualities, free from the disturbing presence of recent accumulations. Samatta is developed by cultivating an awareness, a mindfulness of everything that arises. In the meditation session we relax the body, speech and mind and rest naturally and simply in the present state which is by nature free from all the obstacle-delusions of desire, anger, ignorance, jealousy and pride.

The second aspect has two stages: the ordinary stage and the extraordinary stage The ordinary stage concerns the mind that we are developing in our sitting practice. The state which we are trying to cultivate in our beginners' samatta practice is not just a blank, blind stillness and quietude. It is a state wherein there can arise an *awareness of the clarity and qualities of mind* - these qualities being recognized by mind itself. This is called the ordinary second aspect of meditation. The extraordinary stage of this second aspect covers not only this naturally-clear mind resting within itself and within an understanding of its own clarity, but also the *presence of Bodhicitta* - Bodhicitta free from the triplistic veil of subject, object and action as separate entities. 'Who is meditating?' 'Meditating upon what?' 'Meditating in which way?' and other such notions and biases are transcended.

The third aspect of meditation concerns practicing the above with *completely proper motivation* so that the ordinary and extraordinary stages of meditation are supported by, guided by, the motivation to benefit all beings and accompanied by the great openness of loving-kindness and compassion. The result of such meditation is a Mahayana result. It is the motivation that makes the difference between the meditations of the Hinayana and Mahayana which are otherwise very similar. Impartial calm meditation, rich in awareness of itself and beyond triplicity, and based upon an altruistic motivation - that is full realization. The moment that such realization is achieved there will be spontaneous activity to benefit beings; effortless and all-accomplishing.

The realization that emerges through the Hinayana practice is very similar to that achieved by the Buddha but it does not have the qualities and activity to benefit others. It is an incomplete realization of the ultimate truth; a realization which is very dry - dry of compassion and dry of the full activity of the perfect Buddhas. It is a realization of the ultimate truth - but not 'just as it is'. For this reason whenever we do tranquillity meditation, a visualization or *tong.len,* we practice it in the following stages:

* First our mind must be ready to meditate; it must be pacified. (Most of the Hinayana practitioners want to do this too.) This putting the mind into a suitable disposition is usually accomplished by concentrating upon the breathing process, cultivating mindfulness of walking, developing awareness of body sensations and so on. There are objective and non-objective techniques.

* As a result of the above the mind becomes peaceful - a sort of

'blank-peaceful' to which clarity has to be added. (At this stage, not the innate clarity of mind itself - that can only emerge through realization. Just lucidity.)

* The calmness and clarity are then to be set within a framework of right motivation - the wish to help others. Once this is accomplished the meditation is full meditation. Just blank meditation makes us feel relaxed and comfortable and will free us temporarily from nervousness. There are no results beyond this.

If we do Vajrayana practices, visualizations and so forth, without the enlightening motivation of Bodhicitta, then we are just going through another trip. There will be more benefit from visualizing a deity than from visualizing a complicated rock but there will never be the full results without Bodhicitta motivation - even though that deity represents the ultimate truth.

### *Prajna (Wisdom)*

The three aspects of prajna are ordinary samsaric wisdom, lesser transcendent wisdom and highest transcendent wisdom. The first covers all the many sorts of *worldly wisdom* which we used to call' art' in Tibet, all the studies of which are covered by ten topics, five of which are minor, and five of which are major. The five minor disciplines are: poetry (and rhetoric), astrology, terminology (including grammar), dramatic art and etymology.

*Poetry* means the expression of things in a pleasant way and in a way that enables others to feel as we do, even if they are not in that particular situation themselves.

*Astrology* is the study of the inter-relationship of the various bodies of the universe. The way that we exist internally is a total true reflection of the way that outer things exist. This is why a charting based upon a correlation of the outer elements at our birth can show exactly and undeniably the sort of mother and father we have and so forth. The outer universe is the outer body and our earth its inner body. This human body is an outer body and within it are the subtle bodies and then all the aspects of mind. There are many bodies and they all have connections with one another. The study of these connections is astrology. An example of this is our calendar. Sometimes there are thirteen months in the year, sometimes only eleven. Sometimes there are twenty-eight days in the month and sometimes there are thirty. Why? because we regulate our calendar according to the cycles of the moon in a way which allows no mistake for the seasons. Our summer months are always summer months and the winter months always winter months. Eclipses of the sun and moon, everything, is clearly described by astrology and can be charted in the calendar. There are several systems of astrology. There is 'white' astrology and 'black' astrology; nothing to do with white magic and black magic or good and bad. The black astrology is more complicated and mathematical, involving angular calculations and so forth, while the white astrology is a simpler form.

*Terminology and grammar* deals with the use of terms in order to express ideas. For Tibetan language there were originally seven master treatises giving the rules for language but unfortunately five were lost. However, these two contained all the information of the other five and so Tibetan grammar is complete.

*Dramatic art* incorporates many things and covers many topics. It can be used to portray history or as a means of expression and it involves pretending; pretending whatever it is that we wish to portray. If it is an historical drama then we reproduce as faithfully as possible the historical event - the personalities of the people involved, their background and the historical facts. Theatre is like poetry since the people watching it are transported to that condition, that realm, that situation by the motion and imagery of the players. It utilizes movement, music, singing - many things.

*Etymology* is a loose name for the fifth of the lower studies. It deals with names. Names are used for everything; some of them are meaningful and exist through reason while others are meaningless. When, for instance, we say *sang-jay* in Tibetan, our word for Buddha, it implies 'sang' - 'awakened' from the sleep of ignorance, and 'jay' - 'full blossoming' of all the qualities and knowledge. There is another sort of name which has no meaning: house, for example. A house is just called a house - a sound grew up in association with that object. There is a whole text which contains hundreds of names, many for each thing, showing how a flower can be called 'that which drinks through its feet' or 'that which has fine petals' and so on.

The above five topics are known as the five lesser disciplines and they deal with less important topics. The five greater disciplines are: crafts, medicine, communication, truth and dialectics.

The first of these is *the study of how to create and how everything was created.* The whole universe is made of five component elements, five qualities of nature which support one another thereby enabling the universe to exist as it is. Even when we make a pot, it is possible without a teacher to learn how everything is composed. We need clay (solidity), water to make it wet (humidity), air to propel it, space in which it moves and heat to make it usable. We have gained insight into the five elements by simply making a pot. This branch of the greater disciplines or sciences covers metalwork, woodwork, weaving, pottery and a host of other creative activities.

Second is *medicine.* In craft we learn how everything is created. In medicine we study how it functions. When the functioning goes wrong, we apply the correct treatment and it works again. There are many ways of diagnosing the problem when the human body goes wrong. In Tibet, if a good doctor was unable to diagnose the problem immediately then, if there were ten possible sicknesses with ten potential cures, he would take ten small pots and place a sample of the patient's urine in each. To each was added one of the ten medications and by skilful observation of what happened the doctor could tell which remedy to apply. The medications are chemical; chemical in the broadest sense of the term, that is, a composition of naturally occurring things. Tibetan medicines were closer to nature than Western ones. The organs of the human body have specific qualities and attributes which correspond to similar qualities in herbs in the outer world and those herbs can be picked and applied carefully to cure the organs of beings. That is basically how Tibetan medicine works.

The study of *communication* covers many things. It is often considered to be just the study of the Sanskrit alphabet but it is much more than that. It requires a study of all the elements, movement, feelings, the environment, the atmosphere and so on. Someone who develops this understanding of communication or sound can hear and comprehend the language of animals, who may not have language in the same sense that we do but who do make sounds to express certain things. In a similar way, we can understand the language of the wind or of fire burning, water running and so forth.

Movements make sound. One part of this knowledge is being presently developed in the form of an understanding of the theories which have given rise to television, radio and the telephone, enabling us to talk to someone on the other side of the planet just as though that person were in the same room as ourselves. It is the use of movement, the environment and sound.

*Truth* means the study of what is validly perceived and what is not. It is often translated as logic. Logic is one way of determining the truth. Buddhist philosophical logic is very complicated and the specialized section of *dialectics* is hard to master. One needs ten or fifteen years of determined practice to be able to do it properly.

Thus first we learn how everything is made, then how it functions, then the inter-relationship of everything and finally the truth about that. These five lesser and five greater sciences comprise worldly wisdom.

*Lower transcendent wisdom* covers both the relative and absolute levels of truth but from a one-sided approach, wherein killing and the other non-virtues are bad and suffering is very bad. To do the positive things is good and happiness and altruism are very good. All takes place within the realm of duality. Even the ultimate is the opposite of the relative. It transcends samsara but is the lower aspect of the wisdom that transcends samsara.

*The highest non-samsaric wisdom* is the wisdom of non-duality. This is the pure essence of Madhyamaka, beyond words, imagination or explanation. To know the way things work is thus the first stage (samsaric wisdom). To know the way they really are is the second stage and to know that which is truly the essence of everything is the third stage. This third stage can only be described very roughly and unclearly - it needs to be tasted. We have to taste it.

When we practice the path of the Bodhisattva, we practice according to the six paramitas. Having three aspects each, there are thus eighteen aspects of practice to accomplish and we develop them from their beginnings until they truly become paramitas or perfections. In doing this we traverse the five paths of the Bodhisattva - the paths of accumulation, preparation, insight, familiarization and fulfilment. As we make this journey, the ultimate of the first path becomes the relative of the second path, and the ultimate of the second path becomes the relative of the third path and so on until the fifth path.

The first stage of profound Bodhisattva realization is achieved with the third path and this grows profoundly through ten stages. Until the tenth stage, although there will be a growth in actual realization and understanding, there is still the obstacle of subject and object. There is not full Buddhahood. At the last level of the tenth stage there is full realization of the transcendent ultimate truth itself, by itself, just as it is. That is the non-dual wisdom which we call the Buddha. That wisdom from the end of the tenth stage to Buddhahood is called the Vajra-like wisdom - indestructible, unobscurable wisdom.

We should understand what the Mahayana means, its fundamental principles - the Bodhicitta, compassion and the results of Mahayana practice - understand the qualities of the Bodhisattvas and Buddhas and what realization really means. It was not that there was first the Buddha and that then we named him as being the realization of the ultimate truth. The realization of the ultimate truth is always there. He who achieves such realization is a Buddha.

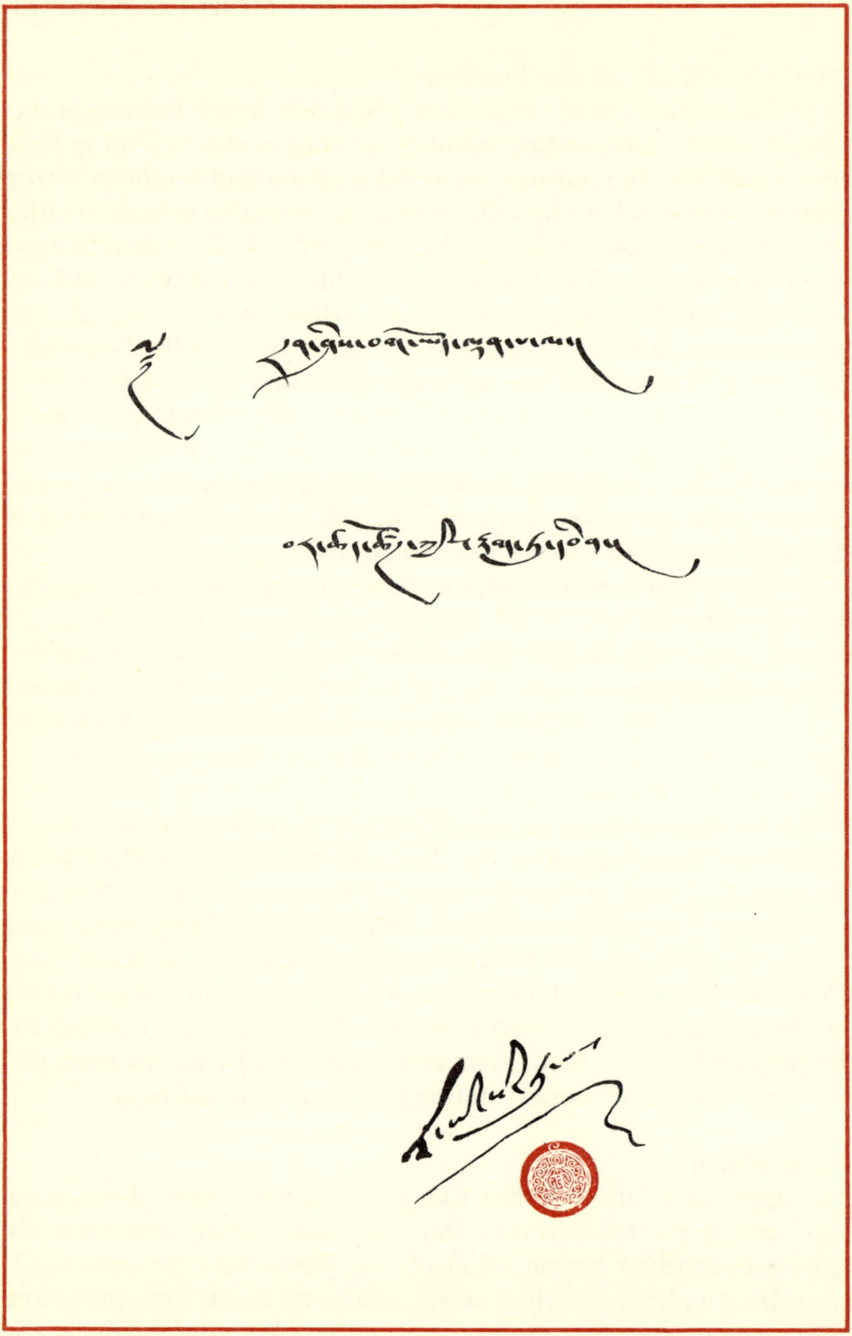

# The Seven Points Of Mind Training

## Introduction

All of the Buddha's teaching falls within the two aspects of Hinayana and Mahayana. The Mahayana itself has two aspects: the Sutrayana and the Tantrayana. All those teachings are there to help us abandon the notion of self-entity and what we shall now study is the Mahayana approach known as *lo-djong* or Mind Training, which removes the delusion of self and develops the Bodhicitta in the form of a very living compassion and all that is necessary for the cultivation of that compassion. *Lo* means mind or thought and *djong* means to practice, train or purify. This name is given to the practice because we use its techniques to transform the present relative level of being, which is obscured by the ego or 'I-notion', into the unobscured mind of truth - just as it is.

Through the notion of 'I' we tend to accumulate that which is negative; by 'negative' we mean that which is unwanted, the causes of suffering. At present we feel that an ego exists and we act and relate to things according to its existence. Application of the Mind Training techniques enables us to use the obstacles themselves as a means of working towards the pure mind. The pure mind itself was never affected by those obstacles and when we reach that ultimate level it is as it always was. Until then it is very necessary to work on the relative level by training and purifying the obscured mind.

How can we use the obscurations to purify themselves? If we consider this ego then, as the Buddhist teaching and philosophy demonstrates very clearly, it is normally the thing which builds up the possibility for all the obscuring factors to arise; it creates the space for their existence. However, this very same notion of ego can, when we know how, become the seed of realization. We know what we want and what we do not want. We know when we are happy and unhappy; thus we can understand how others can feel happy or unhappy. We can understand their suffering. Applying how 'I' feel to others can give birth to compassion and as compassion develops it becomes the relative Bodhicitta - to wish others to be happy and to forget oneself in order to bring them happiness. Of course, it is impossible to abandon self-interest immediately, but we can start with small things such as giving to those who are poor and hungry, or accepting abuse because we know the other person is angry and out of control. Step by step the relative Bodhicitta will emerge and return ever closer to its essence until it becomes the ultimate Bodhicitta, which is itself finely polished and cultivated until it becomes full realization. Thus through the application of Mind Training, the ego becomes the seed of liberation rather than the seed of samsara and suffering. It is very important to realise that Mind Training is not something adopted from the outside - it means learning to use that which is already within us. We need to discover it and let it unfold.

There are several examples that help us understand how the Mind Training process works. There exists a plant which is a very powerful poison for humans and most animals but which peacocks can eat without harm. In fact it enhances their beauty more than anything else simply because the peacocks have the necessary means to transmute it. Normally, desire, jealousy and anger are powerful poisons but these same poisons' nature can constitute the path to realization if the techniques of Mind Training are applied - that is why it is so important within the Mahayana.

Just to know the techniques is not enough. There must be a readiness or motivation to practice and this comes about through being exposed to the obscurations and their effects. It is like being a lotus. Lotuses do not grow in fountains or ponds where there is nothing but clear water, where all is clean and fresh. That most pure and beautiful thing, the lotus, grows in old and dirty mud-pools. Within those beings who are subject to the bonds and stings of suffering and ignorance, there lies buried the seed of the enlightened mind, the great compassion, and it is easier for them to want to unlock it and let it grow because they are directly exposed to the misery of its non-development and to the need for the benefits of its growth.

The great masters and highly-realized beings always explain the path of love and compassion in many different ways and from many points of view. It is both meaningful and important. One short verse by Nagarjuna says:

*Beings who want to get rid of suffering*
*Must get rid of the causes of suffering*
*Rather than the suffering itself.*
*For them to rid themselves of the causes of suffering*
*They must believe others to be more important than themselves.*
*That is the method that leads them away from suffering,*

*But in order to be completely free from suffering*
*They must attain the great liberation.*
*The root of that great liberation is Bodhicitta*
*Which must be, from the very beginning,*
*Firm and stable like the largest of mountains.*

On this mountain will grow all the things necessary for liberation, especially an impartial unrestricted compassion. At present our compassion is quite restricted, being easy to engender when we are happy and almost non-existent when we are faced with problems. Unrestricted compassion is immutable and it is directed towards absolutely all beings within the cycle of existence, whether they be friend, enemy or stranger. At the very end of the Bodhicitta journey, however, when we come to the very essence of ourselves and everything, then the last step can only be made through a wisdom that has left behind even this immutable impartial compassion. Why? because that compassion has grown through an understanding that no one wants to suffer; their wish for happiness and dislike for suffering are the same as our own. Thus we do everything we can, offering our body, speech and mind to bring them temporary and lasting happiness and to free them from suffering. Because *we* are trying to help *them*, there is still duality. To realize fully the full qualities of the Buddha-nature, the as-it-isness or the absolute truth, this dualistic compassion has to be left behind.

The Mind Training practice is dealt with through seven steps or stages. *The Seven Points of Mind Training* is a teaching which comes from the great master *Atisha*. Atisha studied Mind Training and Bodhicitta under three gurus: Dharmakirti, Dharmarakshita and yogin Maitreya. Through the Mind Training practice Dharmakirti had achieved realization and even while developing it he was able to benefit many beings. Expressing his joy in practice he was truly able to take their sufferings to himself, cure their diseases and establish them on the path. The Mind Training teaching passed from Dharmakirti to Atisha and Atisha took it to Tibet. From Atisha until the present day these teachings have been handed down in an unbroken lineage of transmission. I myself received these teachings from His Holiness the XVIth Gyalwa Karmapa. Although we trace these teachings back to Dharmakirti, they are completely based upon the instructions of Sakyamuni Buddha, belonging to the sutra level of practice.

The actual seven points are:

1. basic preliminary practice - the foundation,
2. the main body of the practice: the two aspects of Bodhicitta - relative Bodhicitta and ultimate Bodhicitta,
3. use of negative circumstances as part of the path to realization,
4. application of the practice to all aspects of one's life,
5. the measure of Mind Training,
6. the vows or commitments of Mind Training (what one should not do) and
7. the precepts of Mind Training (the things one should do).

## The First Point: the Preliminary Practices

The preliminary practices are so-called because they are done first. They are often called the *four ways of changing the mind* or four basic contemplations. The first of these concerns the precious human existence, an appreciation of what our life is truly worth; how it is not something to be wasted because it is the very thing that can bring us to an understanding of the meaning of all life, the essence of life. It is a very valuable and worthwhile asset. Just to understand the preciousness of the human existence is not in itself enough - the human life must be made precious, used to the full.

Even though the human life can be made very precious, it is extremely fragile and it will not last forever. It is *impermanent.* From the very instant of birth its span is ever decreasing. Birth is also the start of the possibility of death and when that death will come is something no one can say. A doctor may say that one will not die of a certain disease within a certain time but no one can guarantee that during that time death will not take place. An appreciation of life's transience stimulates us to make full use of it and meditation upon death actually makes us appreciate life. Just to know that death will come is not enough. We must study what will happen to our mind once this flesh and blood body dies; how what we have created in this life through our actions of body, speech and mind, has created positive and negative *karma,* karmic tendencies which will accompany us after the physical death. Those karmic potentials are never lost; they do not just fade away. They ripen when conditions are correct and produce experiences, good or bad, according to whether the karmic act was positive or negative. The experience emerges from the karmic potential itself. Nothing else is required. This is why, in this world, this field of karmic ripening, even though everyone wants happiness and no one wants suffering, there is nevertheless so much suffering. People's happiness and suffering does not arise from their immediate efforts but from the ripening of karma. This explains why some try with millionfold effort to achieve little and fail, while others achieve everything with hardly any effort.

When we realize that karma works in such a way, it is not just an academic observation. Karma will affect us. However, just as the karmic seeds are within us, so is their antidote and so is the means to escape the karmic consequences we have created. The means is within us but it does not operate automatically. It has to be put into operation very properly otherwise there will be no change; things will continue as they are now , maybe becoming better, maybe becoming worse.

If we do not deal with the latent karmic potentials, they will ripen into their pleasant and unpleasant results bringing about the *sufferings of samsara.* If we think clearly and carefully about the world in which we live we can see and experience the whole process of suffering. We can think of those who have nothing trying to get something - happiness, wealth, health or anything. Those who have something arc looking for more. Those who have sufficient are suffering to preserve and guard what they have. In the end each will lose whatever he has, since when death comes it is impossible to take even one single possession along with one; even this precious body of which we are so fond, of which we take such great care, and to which we are so attached, we will have to leave behind.

It is vital for us to know the way in which these preliminary contemplations of the precious human life, impermanence, karma and suffering are ordered and linked. It is not just a philosophical arrangement of ideas, concocted by thinkers. It is a true reflection of the actual nature of the world. Being so fundamental, it makes the main part of the first part of Mind Training. Because life, the world, is like that then we must awaken the inner means mentioned above and follow the path that leads us out of samsara. In doing the right things we will take ourselves away from samsara - but what are the right things? We can discover them through treading the path of knowledge and discovery taught by the Buddha. Thus our first step is a homage to the Buddha, Dharma and Sangha: taking refuge. In one way this homage and refuge is an appeal for help when we are helpless as well as a reverence; a token of respect. However it is much more than that.

Taking refuge in the *Buddha,* besides being a homage to Sakyamuni, is a recognition of, and homage to , our own Buddha-nature as well as the aim to achieve the realization of a Buddha. Had we been able to do everything to achieve that aim by ourselves, then it all would have been over a long time ago. We are still here. We have to travel a path, the path of *Dharma,* the direct teaching of how to become Buddha. This is the path that many thousands of great masters have practiced and by which they achieved full realization. To follow that path is the real homage to the Dharma. But just to read books and practice could do as much harm as good; we might get quite hurt. We need to follow the path under the guidance of a being who has confidence, as well as the compassion to help us, and who is properly experienced. To follow such guidance is the real homage to the *Sangha.* This triple homage to Buddha, Dharma and Sangha is known as the *refuge.*

Even refuge in the sense of trusting the Buddha-nature, the path and our teacher and using them to rid ourselves of suffering and find true happiness is not enough; it is one step. The next step is compassion and *Bodhicitta.* Thus the whole of the preliminary practice, point one of the Mind Training, becomes as follows: we come to a heartfelt understanding of the four basic contemplations - of our precious life, impermanence, karma and suffering - and then when we really feel it and mean it, we pay our homage to the Triple Gem (Buddha, Dharma and Sangha) and awaken our Bodhicitta. Then we are prepared to enter the second stage, the practice of relative and ultimate Bodhicitta.

## The Second Point: Actual Bodhicitta Practice

Bodhicitta is developed in two phases:

1. relative Bodhicitta practice and
2. ultimate Bodhicitta practice.

The first of these, the relative Bodhicitta, is practiced in three stages:

a. preparation
b. main body of the practice and
c. conclusion.

### *1a. Preparation*

Any meditation that we do is a method, a means, to help us gain a direct experience of the Tathagata nature. The practice of these means will eventually bring us to the point where there is direct realization of what Tathagata nature really is, but in order to reach that point we need first to train ourselves in meditation and the initial step we must take is to learn how to concentrate, how to keep our mind constantly on one object. To see something clearly we first have to focus upon it. To see our reflection in a bowl of water we should not touch it but let it be still. To see the nature of our mind, which is the essence of the universe, we first have to learn to approach it and let the mind itself settle. In the beginning there are many obstacles, many disturbances caused by all sorts of thoughts. If we have no means of calming the mind and making it peaceful then we will not be able to go very far. This is why we practice samatta meditation. The samatta meditation given in this preparatory stage is a very simple technique employing one's own breath.

Sitting on a comfortable cushion, we let our thoughts come and go, neither trying to stop them arising nor being carried away by them. Not bothering with thoughts and just leaving them to come and go as they will, we concentrate on the breath itself. After letting the body, mind and breath relax into a natural state for some minutes, we then count the breath...one, two, three, four and so on...up to twenty-one. After the twenty-one breaths we pray, reciting the homage to the Triple Gem and then the four immeasurable contemplations.

### *1b. The Main Body of the Practice*

The main body of relative Bodhicitta practice in Mind Training is the tong.len, or taking-and-sending meditation. Tong means to send and len means to take (Tib.) The starting point of this taking-and-sending utilizes those things with which we have the strongest emotional links in this life. These are then extended until the practice embraces all sentient beings.

The person who is closest to us in this life is our mother and we vizualize her standing before us. As we exhale we feel that all our happiness and all our causes of happiness go to her, totally. She really receives them. When we inhale we really think that we are taking all of her suffering and the causes of future suffering. We work like this until we feel that we can give her all our happiness and that we are perfectly willing to take all her suffering; then we go a little deeper. The happiness that we now offer her is every happiness we will encounter until we reach the Great Liberation - the state which transcends happiness and suffering. Every aspect of her suffering, down to the very root - the ego- we take to ourselves.

Once we feel ready to give our mother everything, we extend the practice to others who are important to us: friends, brothers, sisters and so on. Then we extend it to those friends and acquaintances who are not so important to us but about whom we feel good. Then we extend it to strangers, then to enemies, and then to those enemies we really detest. After that we apply it to all beings. We apply the practice to the easiest person first and then gradually extend it to the most difficult. Then when we say or pray, "I want to benefit others", it means much more than just a shove of help. It means you want to benefit them just as a medicine does when they are sick; just as a road does, helping them to go where they want whether it is rain or shine; just as food brings them nourishment; just as a bridge helps them cross the river and so on. There is nothing we are not prepared to do to help them, and just like medicine, the road, the food and the bridge, we expect nothing in return for our help.

### *1c. Conclusion*

This stage of relative Bodhicitta is concerned with developing evenness and impartiality in everyday reactions. Forms, tastes, sounds and so on, everything has an effect on us. When we taste something delicious then a pleasant feeling arises. When we touch something soft then a pleasant feeling arises. Our reactions to the sense impressions is either pleasant, unpleasant or neutral. When we have pleasant feelings then attachment usually follows. When we have unpleasant feelings then aversion, sometimes even hate, wells up and when there are neutral feelings then a form of ignorance ensues. At first we must work with the reactions which are easiest for us to practice upon and we extend this gradually to encompass everything.

At this point it is useful to explain an aspect of the six realms which makes things easier to understand. As humans we have within us all the feelings of the six realms. Happiness, the feeling of delight in our life, is the god realm. Jealousy is the feeling of the *asuras* (demi-gods). The desire and search for happiness is the human feeling while the dullness and ignorance is the animal within us. The meanness is the *preta* (deprived spirit) aspect and hatred and anger are the hell-realm within us.

In the time between meditation sessions, during our worldly life, all of the six realms will manifest: desire for what we like, aversion for what is unpleasant and so forth. As we come to recognize this process taking place we try to develop impartiality and equanimity, first for the situations that are easiest and then with the stronger more passionate circumstances, until in the end we have this 'sameness' for everything.

## Ultimate Bodhicitta Practice

This has three sections: preparation, main body of practice and conclusion, with an additional section on post-meditation practice.

### *2a. Preparation*

This is similar to the preparatory practice for relative Bodhicitta. We start with refuge and Bodhicitta followed by the seven-branch prayer. The seven branches are prostration, offering, rejoicing in the virtue of others, regretting our own misdeeds, requesting the Buddhas and Bodhisattvas to teach ('turn the wheel of Dharma'), requesting them to live long for the sake of beings, and dedicating the positive outcome of all prayers to the good of all beings. After the seven-branch prayer we do the same concentration meditation (counting the breaths) followed by the taking-and-sending practice.

### *2b. Main Body of the Practice*

This is itself in several parts, the first of which is the meditation upon the not-true-existence of external phenomena. Commencing with the phenomena that we see and feel around us, we apply the philosophy and understanding of the Madhyamaka and Prajnaparamita to understand their absence of true independent identity and we can see them as being just like what we experience in dreams. Once we can see them like that, we extend them to our country, our planet and eventually the entire cosmos.

The next step is meditation upon the non-existence of the inner perceiving mind. Starting from the simplest level, we try to find what we mean by 'I' and 'mine'. Of course if someone asks "Who are you?" we will tell them our name. But if we really investigate from the outside inwards, layer by layer through every part of our body until we reach the heart, we will never find the 'I' as a solid thing to which we can point and say, "This is me". Then since we are sure that 'I' exists and now that we have discovered that it is not physical, we have to investigate space and time to find it. It is not in the past since that has gone already, and it is not in the future because that has not yet happened. What then is the present 'I'? This present is an exceedingly short time: it is not this year, this month, this week, today, this hour, this minute, or even this second. It is much less because it has to be the shortest unit of time. However short a time unit one makes, it must have earlier and later aspects, otherwise there could be no time continuity composed of a chain of such instants. If it can be decomposed into past, present and future segments, then it is not the shortest unit. This process can be applied through either common sense or mathematics and it leads us to deduce that there is no smallest unit of time. If there is no smallest unit of time, then how can the larger units exist, which are supposedly multiples of smaller units? Thus we analyse time and space and discover their voidness. Nothing of time, space or phenomena can be found as true existence - but still there is mind. Thus we discover that mind is something which transcends all these things we have examined and our search will lead us to a discovery of Buddha-nature. We must go that far.

The third step shows us how to be one with the universal essence, the nature of all phenomena, which is in itself something totally beyond our conceptualisation. At first we learned to see things as a dream. This is a remedy for taking the world too solidly, for believing in its independent existence. Then we investigated the sunyata, or voidness of everything, which is the remedy for belief in a self or an 'I'. Both of these practices are antidotes and we need to free ourselves from the power of the antidotes themselves.

If things are like a dream and *sunyata*(voidness) applies so universally but mind is still nevertheless there, thinking and feeling, then what accurate description of mind can we give? In Tibetan it is said "sNang.SZin.gSal.Ba.gSal.SZin.sTong.Pa" which means that there are appearances which we experience with great clarity and that that clarity is in itself sunyata. The sunyata is completely unbroken, unimpeded and universal. Since it is like that, then the way to rest in the essence of mind is just to let the mind be, let the mind rest in its own nature without taking anything from it or trying to add anything to it; without expecting anything from thoughts or seeing them as obstacles to meditation. There is no need to suppress thoughts or to encourage them, inflating them into daydreams. Just to live in the immediate present.

Thoughts are liberated within the Tathagata nature. Meditation on ultimate Bodhicitta is like Mahamudra meditation. The pure state of mind abides on the level of as-it-isness. Thoughts will arise within this state and they will disturb us but we do not have to push them back; if we do we are trying to push back the mind itself. Even though we may not be able to find the mind, it is nothing more than the thoughts - they are like the waves on the mind. Thus we neither follow them nor try to suppress them and we are only concerned with being in the present.

It is said in the Hinayana, Mahayana, and Tantrayana that beginners should start with short meditation sessions, many of them. As the practice deepens they can be extended. So at first we do ten minutes meditation, followed by five minutes rest, then another ten minutes and so on. It will develop by itself.

### *Concluding Phase*

Were we only to meditate on the nowness, it would be profound meditation but would not produce the full Mahayana result, because meditation has to be backed up by compassion. So after the ultimate Bodhicitta meditation we dedicate the meditation to all beings, in the way of the Mahayana, and we take the Bodhisattva commitment; just as before the meditation, we perform the refuge, Bodhicitta and seven-branch prayer.

### *Post Meditation Instructions*

It is very necessary to maintain the awareness that we develop during meditation practice, carrying it through to the post-meditation phase; the time in-between sessions. The way in which we do this is:

*...by the illusory yogi relating with an understanding*
*of illusion to this illusory world...*

If we apply this maxim to tantric practice, for example, then we speak in terms of vajra body, vajra speech and vajra mind, meaning that after we have finished the actual meditation session upon a certain visualized Buddha-form, we keep the presence of body, speech and mind that we have discovered in that meditation and extend it into our daily life, with a great feeling of vajra-confidence in the presence of the deity (the body aspect), the mantra power (speech aspect) and the quality of profound wisdom (the mind aspect). This extension of practice into daily lives is known as living *the three vajras.*

Whatever we do after the meditation session - talking, eating, pleasant or difficult situations - we try to keep the same depth of understanding that we have discovered in our absolute Bodhicitta practice.

### *Summary of Second Point*

When we apply this second point we sit in a good posture, our back straight, and go through each stage of the relative and ultimate Bodhicitta practice as shown, doing each as clearly and vividly as we can. When doing the samatta meditation, we place our hands on our knees and our breathing should be relaxed and completely natural. When saying the prayers of refuge, Bodhicitta and dedication, we hold the hands folded at the heart, the fingers slightly open at the top. During the stage where we search for the self, we do so relaxedly, not with anguish or tension; and when we are just sitting letting thoughts come and go, we let thoughts pass as though they were bubbles streaming through water.

## The Third Point-Utilizing Negative Circumstances as Part of the Path to Realization

There are many sorts of negativity but we can formulate two basic categories: negativity arising from the outer vessel - the universe- and negativity arising from the inner content of that vessel- the sentient beings. The first of these categories is that of all the uncomfortable imbalances of the elements such as fire, flood, sickness and so on. The second is all the unpleasantness emanating from beings, such as them being angry with us or making life difficult. Sometimes what they do is the result of former negativity and sometimes it is a fresh cause of negativity because it can spark off the reactions of desire, anger, ignorance, jealousy or pride within us.

Whatever the circumstances, whether they will be positive or negative for us when they arise depends upon our understanding, not just upon the circumstances themselves. If we cannot cope with the situation skilfully, they are negative. If we have the understanding and skill to transmute the circumstances into fuel for our practice, then they are positive. For example, should someone be aggressive towards us and we retaliate, the whole situation is negative. However, if we understand what is happening to be the ripening of our own karma and that the karma has appeared in this outer manifestation as aggression, then we can just accept what is happening with love and forbearance, realizing it to be a means of purifying that particular karma.

This does not mean going out into the streets and inviting aggression so that we can purify our past karma. There are some sufferings that we can avoid and others that we cannot. Normally we spend a lot of time and effort avoiding sufferings, even the tiniest suffering, but when we encounter an unavoidable suffering then we have to recognize it as a ripening of karma and accept it joyfully, knowing that the ripening of karma is in itself the remover of the cause of that karma and that it had to occur some time or another. At the time of karmic ripening, the skilful practitioner applies one of the techniques for purifying the karma and utilizes its presence to the full. Without such an approach, people react negatively to adverse conditions and sow the seeds of more karma. This is just how the samsaric cycle works - constant negative action and reaction perpetuating and recreating worldly existence. Realization is nothing in itself; nothing more than a release from the vicious circle of samsara and that is why breaking the pattern of negative reaction constitutes part of the path to realization. Through removing any new cause of samsara and by purifying the already existing karma, we can re-find the true nature of our mind, of ourselves. Such practices as the Vajrasattva meditation are powerful means for purifying existing karma but it is not practical to do them all day long and to maintain the visualization while doing our daily work. Since this is the case, the natural purification of simply accepting the sufferings which we cannot easily avoid is important.

Since beginningless time we have not really understood which actions are harmful to us and others, and which are beneficial. Everything became food which fed the ego and our everyday happiness or sufferings are the products of former good or bad karma respectively. Not knowing this, we take success and happiness to be the fruit of our immediate efforts and use thoughts about this to boost the concept of ego. When we are suffering we react, in retaliation or self-pity and so forth, and this also boosts the ego-illusion. Happiness and suffering both cause the ego to develop rather than diminish it and the ego is the very seed of suffering. Shantidéva says that all the suffering throughout existence stems from the ego. The ego is the real demon that persecutes us; a completely non-existent demon since, no matter how hard we search, it can never be found as anything. Nevertheless, once the illusory belief in a self has been created then that 'I' desires its happiness, resents suffering and is ignorant of the actual way in which true happiness can be found. Thus 'I' gives rise to the three root poisons of desire, aversion and ignorance and these in their turn give rise to the sufferings of samsara. They will never be annihilated until their essence, the ego, is uprooted. Until that time they will manifest endlessly. All the sufferings we have at present are the result of our own past unskilful attempts to satisfy the ego or protect it from unhappiness.

When trouble comes our way, we should be sure that its root cause is not the immediate person or situation but our own former karma. If we did not have the karma to be hurt, it could never happen, and the karma that caused the situation, as well as the present ability to be affected by it, all hinge upon the ego. We have been the slave of the ego-delusion for billions and billions of aeons in so many different ways, and now we must make a revolution to overthrow that ego-belief. We could search for the means for making our revolution successful ourselves, but it is not necessary and we might not be successful. It may be very difficult. Dharma is there; the whole path is already very clearly laid out. All the guidance, understanding and means of purifying and removing the ego-belief are available to us.

We have to destroy the ego-belief; egotism is our worst enemy. Human or animal enemies may hurt us but the very worst that they can do is to kill us. It seems terrible but death is not that serious once one understands it. The mind can no longer inhabit one body and so it takes another, according to the power of karma. Whereas physical enemies can only kill us, the ego-enemy has dominated and determined our existence for countless ages. Now that we have the very rare and special opportunity of a precious human existence, we must use it for the right purpose - for the great destruction of ego. It is not that the ego is bad - that we should hate it and fight it. It is a pointless delusion that has caused trouble and its removal comes through understanding, penetrating through to the essence of existence. We do not need to hate it but use it, to make it the seed of realization and to make ourselves a Son of the Buddha. That is the proper revolution.

If we wish to use life-circumstances as part of our practice in terms of the ultimate truth then we must know them to be dream-like and illusory. Further than this, we see them as the manifestation or play of the four *kayas.* Whatever we see or experience is never something other than Buddha-nature; not something apart from realization, the Buddha's *Dharmakaya.* But through the second-by-second activity of ego, desire and so forth, that pure aspect is hidden, obscured. How can we find the Buddhakayas within these situations? If we investigate that which is happening to us, in a similar way to our step-by-step analysis of the body and mind to find the self, then we cannot find one independently existing atom of reality in it; nevertheless it manifests. Like the manifestations in a dream, there is appearance without origination, the birthless state. That is the birthless *Dharmakaya.*

The circumstances were never born and do not arise from anywhere and yet they are there; we are still talking, eating, getting sick and so on.

The unborn nature does not make them a great blank or hole. The vivid appearance of what is not really there is the *Sambhogakaya* aspect. The simultaneous union of the unborn and the manifest is the *Nirmanakaya* aspect. All these three - Dharmakaya, Sambhogakaya and Nirmanakaya - are not separate things. They are one. That one is the *Svabhavikakaya*. Dharmakaya is the realization which transcends all imagery and qualification. Sambhogakaya is like brilliant sunlight within that Dharmakaya space and Nirmanakaya is like the growth power and energy streaming from that sun. The ultimate level is not something different from ourself. Neither is the relative level.

**The Four Provisions**

There are four things which help us practice both the relative and ultimate Bodhicitta. They are:

* *accumulation* of virtue and wisdom,
* *purification* of the causes of suffering, suffering itself and obstacles,
* *appreciation* concerning the cause of negativity and
* *offering and praise* to the Protectors.

***a. Accumulation***

'Accumulation' is a term applied to our development of the causes of happiness and our creation of the circumstances favourable to enlightenment. Accumulation is equally important as a support for purification.

We all appreciate happiness and dislike suffering. This is a very natural reaction and through it the ideas of positive and negative have evolved. 'Accumulation' means the gathering of the virtuous. To continually increase the amount of virtue we can create and to diminish the non-virtue is the only way that we can ever get rid of suffering. In this way accumulation is the direct cause of happiness but it is not the direct cause of realization because happiness is not realization. Happiness exists because of suffering; it is its opposite pole. Accumulation of virtue removes the relative suffering and this makes the realization of the profound, non-dependent happiness much easier. Having removed the negative we are left with the positive results of our virtue and this itself constitutes an obstacle to realization - a very necessary obstacle. An example which makes this very clear is that of the growth of a seed. By itself, the seed will never grow to produce its fruit. It needs to be planted in the soil, moistened and warmed. The dirt, the water and the heat are the positive obstacles that enable the seed to flourish and evolve into its full possibility. In a similar way, we first create the positive obstacles to be able to remove the negative ones, which are grosser and painful. Then we are in a comfortable position to remove the positive obstacles and benefit from the full development of realization. The positive obstacles are removed by wisdom.

This is not just an idea: this is the way, the very path we must follow. All the teachings of virtue and non-virtue, good karma and bad karma and gathering the accumulations stem from this. If I ask anyone "Do you want to be happy?" then they will of course say, "Yes". Everyone likes that feeling of everything flowing well, of happiness and goodness. But if asked if they really know the causes which will produce that happiness then most people do not know very clearly or certainly. The teachings which illuminate virtue are the light which removes the darkness of uncertainty. Some people grasp them immediately and others are quite dubious. Generally speaking, however, the virtuous practices seem quite reasonable and most people will adopt them. The real accumulation of virtue must be understood to be not just the enactment of the virtuous actions - it is the aware, heartfelt practice of those actions; otherwise, without the understanding and sincere motivation, it just becomes another dream that is not particularly effective in developing the positive.

There are three principal external foci points for our accumulation of virtue:

* The Buddha, Dharma and Sangha are the particular focus of devotional virtue - the virtue of confidence.
* Beings in any realm, whether we can see them or not, who are beset by suffering are the focus of our compassionate virtue.
* Those who have benefited us, or who are well-motivated and good, are the focus of our virtue and respect; this includes our parents, friends, those who have helped us and anyone in the land or entire world who is well-motivated and wholesome.

The way that we cultivate the virtue of confidence is by sincere prostrations, offerings and prayers to the Triple Gem. Also by turning our skills and wealth into devotion, by making beautiful golden Buddha images or offering-lamps and so forth. The very best way of practicing devotional virtue, however, is to offer the mandala because a mandala offered with pure intention is the offering of the entire universe. This is the essence of *tantra* - really simple method that achieves a magnificent result. The pure intention that truly makes the mandala offering as valuable as offering the entire universe is the disposition of Bodhicitta, the power of the Mahayana path.

The final aspect of devotional virtue is total faith and trust in the Triple Gem or towards the Buddha-nature, however one wishes to view it. It is almost impossible to have this at first but we can develop it through such meaningful thoughts as :

> *I dedicate all my virtue to the benefit of all sentient beings that they may be liberated from their sufferings and achieve the ultimate peace, the ultimate truth which is the happiness beyond happiness. To that end I dedicate my body, speech and mind to the quest for ultimate realization.*

When we think in this way we can accept sickness, thinking:

> *If I am sick then may that benefit others. If I am to survive and benefit others through living, then may I live. If I must die, then may I die.*

It means to have a great confidence in practice, a faith and trust in its universal applicability.

***b. Purification***

As we have seen above, there is not only suffering to be removed but also the relative happiness which obscures the deepest realization, the ultimate happiness. The first stage in this process of purification is the removal of the causes of suffering - the negative karma. We must be very certain about the fact that suffering does not just happen without cause. All suffering is the product of negative causes and our immediate concern should be to stop any further creation of causes for future suffering. None of us likes to suffer but instead of fighting the suffering we should attack its causes.

How can we purify the already-created causes of suffering which are yet to manifest, the latent underground seeds within us that could ripen into suffering in the future? The main way is through a sincere and deeply-felt confession of former wrongs. That in itself is sufficient but there are four main powers of purification taught in the scriptures.

There is one good quality inherent to bad actions, even very bad ones such as killing a person. What is this? It is the potential of purification. When the four powers are properly applied then any sin or bad action can be purified, its effects counteracted. These four powers are:

* the power of renunciation,
* the power of turning away,
* the power of reliance and
* the power of remedy.

The *power of renunciation* means to feel very bad about the mistakes we have made; to recognize them as unwholesome and acknowledge them. There must be the feeling that it was definitely not a good thing that we did, that it was bad. The *power of turning away* is a further extension of this, being the resolution never to do the bad actions again. Having realized that we have made a mistake we determine never to repeat it, even at the cost of our lives, if need be. Without this second power, the first is not totally complete because it is only when we think that we never want to do the bad action again that we are certain of our conviction that it really was something bad.

The *power of reliance* lends a support and strength to our regret and resolution. 'Reliance' means to place one's confidence in the absolute and this is accomplished by the refuge and Bodhicitta. By taking refuge in the absolute truth (the Buddha), the path of realization to that truth (the Dharma), and the friends who help us towards that realization (the Sangha), and by developing this into the Bodhicitta (the wish to achieve that realization oneself in order to be of supreme benefit to all sentient beings), we make a very positive basis within which our confession and resolution are deeply meaningful and are made powerful.

The *power of remedy* is to support the preceding factors with *sunyata* (voidness) realization, knowing all good and bad actions to be only relatively manifesting phenomena with no ultimate reality; knowing that the relative karmic causes will produce a relative karmic result within the context of the relative world. The understanding of *sunyata,* the mantras and visualization of the Vajrayana, are all remedies, antidotes, medicines for belief in reality. When, for instance, we vizualize Vajrasattva and the purification takes place through the flow of nectar (or through the flow of light in other visualizations) it is not at all the case that there is an actual nectar or light that has the power to purify. Never! The visualization process is a skilful method which enacts purification but if it were actually the case that real nectar from real Buddhas were actually flowing then we would all have been purified a long, long time ago since there have been Buddhas for countless aeons who could have rained their purification power upon all sentient beings and annihilated samsara. The Buddhas cannot put their purity or wisdom into beings; neither can they take the sufferings of beings to themselves just like that. Even the combined might of all the Buddhas could not do that. What the Buddhas can do is to show us the path and help us to achieve complete realization of the Buddha-nature and thereby remove sufferings and their causes.

These four powers are the specific means that we employ to purify suffering and its causes. They are equally valid for the removal of the more positive obstacles, but in that case they must be accompanied by the prajnaparamita. What does that mean? It means that the purification must take place beyond all duality.

### *c. Appreciation*

This and the following section includes the expression of appreciation towards those who harm us and the dedication of offerings which pacify negative forces. The term 'negative forces' does not only apply to evil influences but very generally to anyone or anything that causes harm to us or creates negative conditions. Why say 'negative conditions'? When someone strikes us and we feel pain then they are creating the negative conditions for that series of events. The root cause for the experience is our own karma which ripens due to these conditions. Our prayers and offerings to the providers of those negative conditions express our gratitude towards them as aids to our practice. There are two stages of such appreciation.

1. When the negative conditions occur, it is of no use to fight them; we must understand them. Having understood them, we then feel grateful that such a situation occurred but we pray that that may be the end of that sort of negative flare-up, which although useful, did present a negative obstacle.

2. The second phase concerns the obstacles created by the ego and unseen forces rather than the immediately frustrating life-circumstances. Since beginningless time all the sufferings and the causes of suffering have been created by the ego - the thought of 'I'. The ego is our worst enemy and our best friend; the worst enemy through creating all the suffering and the best friend because through ego we can start the path to enlightenment. In this phase we appreciate the obstacles created by egotism because working against those obstacles makes the path speedier and more efficient.

When everything is going too smoothly there is the danger of spiritual laziness. The presence of the ego-created obstacles can be a very useful catalyst at such times, spurring us to be sharper, more alert and more diligent. We need to look for any opportunity which may strengthen our practice.

One particular aspect of this section applies to the disturbances that can arise from local deities or spirits when we meditate or do retreat. There are many more beings than just the humans or animals visible to us; they have minds but not the sort of physical existence with which we are able to communicate. When such beings cause strange things to happen, we give them a small symbolic offering made of porridge, called *torma* in Tibetan.

What we say when we make this offering amounts to, "Thank you, thank you very much for the disturbance that you have caused - it helps me understand that there exist things beyond the range of the sights and sounds to which I am accustomed. It brings me that much closer to the'as-it-is'-ness. So thank you, but please do not bother me anymore."

### *d. Offering and Praise to the Protectors*

'Protectors' are those who protect beings on the path to realization; they protect them from obstacles which might impede that path. Therefore we all have the right, the entitlement to their protection. In order to receive it we need to pray to the *Dharmapalas,*(dharma Protectors) requesting them to give all the help we need in order to practice the Dharma path, to achieve realization and help all sentient beings. For other things they will never help. The real essence of these Dharmapalas is one's own faith and trust, supported by the power of compassion. On the relative worldly level there are beings who were formerly very evil and powerful and whom Lord Buddha and Guru Padmasambhava converted. They are now bound by commitment to work for and aid Dharma practitioners. Our responsibility is to request their help for the right purposes and to make the special offerings to them. These are the worldly Protectors. There are non-worldly Protectors, such as Mahakala, in their various forms: Wisdom Mahakalas, Activity Mahakalas and Worldly Mahakalas - many aspects similar to the categories that we make of Dharmakaya, Sambhogakaya and Nirmanakaya. We make offerings to them and request their help on the relative level and cultivate unshakeable faith and devotion towards the ultimate within us, as well as limitless compassion towards all sentient beings on the ultimate level. These are the techniques employed in this stage of Mind Training and they are known as the techniques for integrating negative circumstances into our path. Whenever we are in trouble or sick then we naturally try to do whatever we can to get rid of the problem. We do not need to create, or look for, trouble. The main point of this aspect of the teaching is that we should try to understand the cause of what we are trying to get rid of; why it is happening. When circumstances are good then we also try to understand rather than just immersing ourselves in the pleasure - to be ready to become the king of the entire universe or the poorest, most miserable being ever. With understanding,one is ready for either and either can be accepted with no problem. That is the real acceptance of negative circumstances as part of the path.

## The Fourth Point - Turning One's Entire Life To The Practice

The essence of all the Mind Training instructions is to practice with the five strengths.

*1. The Strength of Intention*

The term employed here (in the Tibetan text) means to 'cast' or to 'launch'. At the very beginning when we awaken the Bodhicitta, we cast our intention towards the ultimate realization and the benefitting of all beings. This initial launch ,or thrust, continues through until the actual realization and benefit are achieved.

*2. The Strength of Habituating Oneself to Practice*

The intention of the first strength is made a reality by the practice of the two modes of Bodhicitta - the relative and the ultimate. These are practiced with stability, diligence and confidence and the increasing presence of this practice is the second strength.

*3. The Strength of Potential*

The potential, or seed, is that of the Buddha-nature. This potential is within all of us and its power is made alive by the awakening positive conditions: the accumulations of virtue and wisdom.

*4. The Strength of Purification and Relinquishment*

From beginningless time until now, and from now until realization is achieved, it is the ego that has caused, and will cause, all the obstacles. It continues second after second, ever re-manifesting according to the laws of interdependence. The conditions which keep the ego alive are the negative conditions. From the time of first understanding this to be the case, up to the time of penetration into the essence of ego, it is still necessary to be selfish, but selfish in a positive way. To wish that we may achieve liberation in order to help beings is positive selfishness while to seek happiness just for ourselves and forget about others is negative selfishness. First, therefore, we need to remove the negative selfishness and, having done this, then we need to remove the positive selfishness. It is very necessary to proceed in such a way, progressively, step by step.

5. *The Strength of Prayer*

The strength of prayer refers principally to the sharing, or dedication, of whatever we have managed to accomplish which was good. We share that virtuous power with all sentient beings and this fifth strength is similar to the first strength, that of motivation: directing the power of what we are doing towards a universal good. This strength also applies to our creation of a right attitude towards negative circumstances. We pray to be able to face them and convert them into something positive and fruitful; to be able to understand them; to be able to appreciate their arisal.

These five strengths indicate how we can integrate the Mind Training approach into our lives. By applying the five strengths as basic principles, all the thousands of facets of everyday life can become useful.

The Mind Training text mentions that the letter HUNG is particularly significant, and that practice involving the HUNG, backed by the five powers, is very complete practice. Each level of our practice, be it Hinayana, Mahayana, or Vajrayana, always needs these five strengths. For example, in our Vajrayana practice we start with refuge and Bodhicitta: this is the first strength. The second strength is the actual visualisation and detailed practice, whichever it may be. The third concerns the offerings and so forth that we make during our sadhana practice. The fourth strength is the absorption into egolessness at the conclusion of the practice; usually this is in the visualisation of absorption of the mentally-created forms and feeling of union with what one has been visualizing. The fifth strength is the concluding dedication. The five strengths apply equally to the Mahayana (as explained above) and the Hinayana - only the motivation is different. In the Hinayana the initial intention is one's own achievement of *anatta* or cessation. The nature of the other four stem from this. The syllable ཧཱུྃ HUNG is mentioned because it is the very essence of everything, the heart. Within the ཧཱུྃ

HUNG are contained all sorts of meditation and skilful practice.

These five strengths also apply to the end of life. No one likes to think or talk about death but we all have to go through the experience. When the karma comes for us to die then we have to accept it, take full advantage of the opportunity. Death is not a punishment. It simply happens. The life, language and feelings to which we have become so accustomed will reach their conclusion at death when mind and body separate. If one is unaware of what is happening then it can be a very horrible experience because one cannot comprehend the various phenomena which occur. If one does understand what is happening then it can be a tremendous opportunity to see the essence, the Buddha-nature, and to achieve some valuable results.

How can one take advantage of this opportunity? The way of correctly transferring consciousness, according to the Mahayana, is through the five strengths.

1. *The strength of potential* is to free our mind from all of its previous worldly preoccupations. The principle obstacles for ordinary people when they die arise through their involvement with their former material wealth, their body, friends, family and so on: name, fame, education, power...all sorts of things. Once we are sure that death is imminent then we must free ourselves from all those concerns by distributing all of the material world that we have accumulated about us, to anyone - our children, religious organizations, the poor - it does not really matter to whom as long as we are freed from all those material things and they can no longer hold us back. This is also the time to say all the things which we meant to say to others, so that those ideas are no longer on our mind.

Then we should try to understand the nature of death; that it is not only about to happen to us but that it happens to absolutely everyone - there are very few people who manage to live for more than one century and they too must die. We are just experiencing that which everyone will experience. It is no big thing. Simply, we can no longer continue to live in this form and we have to leave it, to take another form which will be determined by the actions of this life. We have no choice over the next form of life we will take but we can have some idea of how it will be by analysing our present life, since within it have been created the causes which will shape the future life, just as what we are now was shaped by our past.

An appreciation of the power of karma in shaping our coming existence will lead us to a profound regret for the mistakes that we have made and we confess them really heartfeltly. Except for those who have a really deep insight into Dharma, very few people have a strong and sincere repentence concerning their mistakes. Approaching death will bring such sincerity, since the worldly concerns no longer have any meaning. Even if one were a king with billions of soldiers and atom bombs, and all the worldly power, when death comes there is nothing to strike at, nothing to buy off; one has to die. What one says at that time one really means, and so we confess all our mistakes of this and past lives - totally - and take the commitment never to repeat them. In such a way we do all the aspects of the seven-branch prayer, from prostration to dedication, and it becomes very effective. This is the first stage, that of the potential or seed, which makes the strong background for our dying.

2. Second is the *strength of prayer.* This comes first from the seven-branch prayer, but in this second strength, there is emphasis on paying homage to the Buddhas and Bodhisattvas and to the ultimate truth, praying that in the next life, or in the intermediate state (*bardo*Tib), we may achieve realization of the 'as-it-is'-ness. This is much easier in the bardo than at present. For example, when we dream and recognize the dream state then we can do anything we want. It is much easier because the illusion-aspect is more predominant. Having died, we are freed from the solidity of the life-dream and things can be much more flexible.

There is actually only one dream we need get rid of, the dream of ego. Nothing more than that. Once we have died there is no more body, none of the physical restrictions. The past, present and future can be known, as can other beings' minds. There are many qualities of wisdom because one has awakened from the life-dream. That is why we pray to be able to practice the relative and ultimate aspects of Bodhicitta during the *bardo.* If the prayers are strong then they will work. It is just like when we really want to wake up at a certain time to do something important; we manage because of the power of mind. We will certainly have a stronger motivation than that, as death approaches, and so we make sincere prayers for the bardo state.

3. *The strength of purification.* Since beginningless time all our sufferings have been caused by the ego, by selfishness. Now our approaching death is also due to ego. Ego created all the karmic causes of this body, this place and state of birth, and this death. Created by ego and supported by ego, it will be ego that experiences them. Thus we have to relinquish ego, leave it far behind.

4. *The strength of intention.* During the bardo we are free from the hindrances of this body and this life and mind is just itself. It is a great opportunity for mind to recognize itself, by itself, and this is what we pray for - to be able to achieve realization of mind at the right moment in the bardo.

5. *The strength of habituation* means to practice now so that we will have a strong result later. We should get very used to the Mind Training while we are alive and healthy; it would be a mistake to wait until death is actually approaching - we must start now.

This is how these five strengths of the Mahayana teaching can be useful at the time of death and bring worthwhile results from that situation. On a practical level, there are some things which we can do at the actual time of death which will help, but they are not indispensable. The principal of those explained in the Mind Training text is to lie in the *pari.nirvana* posture when dying. This is not just because that happened to be the posture in which Lord Buddha passed away; it is because of the intimate connection between mind and body, especially concerning *prana.* Prana is everywhere in our body. Present since the moment of conception, it is not restricted to the blood, the muscles or any one physical aspect in particular, although there are certain areas where the panic force is strongest. We learn about prana very properly in the higher tantric instruction which shows how mind is related to body.

The way in which we can die with the pranas well- directed is to lie on our right side with the right hand against the right cheek, the little finger closing the right nostril so that all breathing is done with the left nostril. With the outbreath, we dedicate all our happiness, causes of happiness, virtue, wealth, fame, name, education or anything to the benefit of all sentient beings. With the inbreath we imagine taking to ourselves the sufferings and miseries of all beings; not just as an idea but really meaning it. If we cannot manage to lie in that posture then it is not too important since it is our mind's activity that is most determinant.

The next step is the cultivation of absolute Bodhicitta. This means the understanding that samsara and nirvana - everything - manifests from the Dharmakaya, the Buddha-nature; that on the ultimate level there is no birth or death. They are like closing and opening the eyes. We close the eyes on this life and open them to the next, with the bardo in between. Understanding it in this way there will be no fear. Fear will provoke negative, resentful feelings at the time of death and these are very painful and serve no use. The tong.len exercise described above is practiced up to death itself, and if we are very used to this practice then we will be in a very good position to take advantage of death. At the moment of death itself we absorb the mind in its true nature, absorbing everything into it, just as in meditation we dissolve all the visualisation into the mind nature and rest within it, neither stopping thoughts nor following them. We let the thoughts come and go but the mind itself remains aware of its own nature; aware of itself, by itself. Then death becomes part of meditation. At first the meditation is a little artificial because of the obstacles posed by the body. The death of the body gives a great chance for the liberated mind to recognize itself, its nature. This is the last chance we have.

## Fifth Point - Gauging the Extent of Accomplishment

The Dharma is all the teachings of Lord Buddha and all the explanations of those teachings given by the great masters. The reason that they provided all those instructions for us was to help us remove the obstacles which beset ourselves and all other sentient beings. How efficiently that is achieved is directly dependent upon how much we can get rid of the idea of ego and egotistic reactions. When the ego-delusion is being reduced then we are receiving some benefit; our practice is going in the right direction. When our practice is not diminishing ego, then it is mistaken practice. Because of this it is very necessary for us to keep a constant check on ourselves to make sure that the meaning of our spiritual journey is not lost. Of course we are all selfish to some degree or another but however great or small that selfishness is, it should be diminishing because of our Dharma practice.

One quite simple way to do this is to ask oneself, "If Iwere die tonight would I be filled with regret?" Naturally, everyone will regret losing this precious human existence but one can feel that even though there have been mistakes, one has done one's very best - as much as one could - and one can die with that confidence. If we could not honestly feel that way ourselves at the moment, then from now on it is very important to do as much and as best as we can to understand and train our body, speech and mind; to improve our way of life by applying our understanding to everyday situations and to practice meditation according to the instructions of our spiritual master. If we can do those things then we will reach that beautiful confidence of our life's fullness, feeling that, "If I live for another century then how much more I could achieve, how great - like filling up the ocean. If through some event or another I lose my life tonight, then I have no regret..." Using this sort of thought procedure, one becomes a witness at the scene of one's own life.

When we do encounter negative conditions or feel them arising within ourselves, we can freeze the situation and transform it through the relative and ultimate Bodhicitta. Then nothing can really bother us. Things will still go wrong, and we still avoid the trouble and go for the pleasant things but we are no longer too bothered; everything is comfortable, workable - comfortable when things go well and comfortable when things go wrong. Something negative happens - what joy! without the negative there is no material with which to develop forbearance! In this way everything becomes positive rather than negative and this is what we call the 'great joy'; we move in a circle of joy. It is like when someone knows how to ride well. When the horse is high-spirited and bucks wildly, one does not fall off but enjoys proudly the skill of one's fine horsemanship. When the horse is mild-tempered, one will ride in ease and comfort. We can feel comfortable when everything goes favourably and feel comfortable when surrounded by negative conditions.

There are two things which are very vital to our conduct: dignity and self-respect. *Dignity* means to act before others properly, never doing anything of which we should be ashamed and always acting as purely and beneficially for others as possible. Just dignity, without self-respect, can be very dangerous. Only acting well for the sake of appearances, one can still be very impure inside, like a magnificent, precious crystal vase full of rotting substances. One needs *self-respect,* whereby everything within one is kept as pure as though it were all visible to others; whereby our actions and motivation are heartfelt and not just an immaculate outer show that others trust not knowing what is really within. To have dignity one needs a sense of embarrassment for one's public mistakes and to have self-respect one needs an inner sense of shame for one's failings. We are very complete when we have dignity and self-respect and their presence, as a gauge of our progress, is a pointer to the value of our practice in this life, at death and on into the next life.

We are all impermanent and must die. When we die there is much change and much loss. The continuum of what we are trying to develop in this life is broken. We are like someone who becomes unemployed and who is seeking another job, whose qualifications, proving his skill and education, become very vital. Our dignity and self-respect are proof of the karma we have enacted and, when they are justified, will enable us to die confidently. This is very easy to understand and it constitutes one of the signs of success in, if not completion of, the Mind Training. It is an outer sign.

The full result of Mind Training is deep spiritual realization but that does not mean reaching a point where we can do everything we want. It means that one can cope automatically with any sort of circumstances, reaping the full benefit from the positive and remaining unaffected by the negative; when the situation is positive there is no longer the danger of egotism and pride and when the situation is negative then none of our time or space is given over to it. That is the real accomplishment of Mind Training - to be ready to be the ruler of the universe or the poorest person on earth, at any given moment. No time or space to be proud or depressed or negative. Even when our view is as high as the heavens, our action has to be as fine as powder: fine in the sense of being able to deal with everything in order to help others - even if we are not too bothered about our own achievement.

## Sixth Point - The Mind Training Commitments

The Mind Training implies a certain mode of conduct; there are some things that we ought to do and others that we ought not. This covers three general areas:

a. to practice sincerely without hypocrisy,
b. to behave reasonably and
c. to avoid narrow-minded practice

### *a. Sincere Practice, Free of Hypocrisy*

It is very easy to develop an attitude based on misguided confidence, wherein we feel that, now we are committed to the Mind Training and are part of the Mahayana so it no longer matters what we do or say since it is the mind which is most important. In one way of course, that is perfectly true but it is so easy to develop a no-longer-genuine approach through the space that such an attitude leaves for negativity to be fostered. Even a very great person will find it hard to act sincerely all the time.

Besides acting sincerely, we should bear in mind the effect of our actions upon others. For instance, we may say something that is from the heart and very meaningful for us, without thinking of the impression our honest words will create in the hearer's reality. Or one may be a monk and feel (through reasons of comfort) like wearing lay clothes. Inside one still feels like a monk but other people will judge and formulate opinions based upon the external appearance. Then, even though one's internal behaviour is that of a monk, there is something wrong and whether it is comfortable or not, once one is a monk then one has to behave totally in a way appropriate for a monk, physically, verbally and mentally, no matter what others say.

However, as we cultivate the Mind Training and Mahayana techniques which are quite advanced, it is possible to get into a state of mind where we feel 'I really mean what I am doing and it doesn't matter what anyone else says or thinks', and that is very dangerous. The commitment we have taken is for the relative and ultimate benefit of all beings and that should not be over-ridden by pride or excessive self-confidence. One cannot trust too much what one 'really means'. It is so vitally important to be careful with every action of body, speech or mind and to do the very best one possibly can all the time.

### *b. Behaving Reasonably*

This follows on from the previous point. Our Mind Training should not be allowed to run wild; we must not become wild. Sometimes we come to a point where we feel like that and we will want to act how we wish no matter what people say or what happens to our reputation. If we have given up everything worldly and can be as diligent in our meditation as Milarépa, working incessantly until realization is achieved, then when we achieve the realization we can forget about worldly customs; eat the worst food, wear the worst clothes and just meditate one-pointedly, no matter what people think of us. But, until then, it is a mistake to behave just according to impulse; it becomes just a fascination. We must be very careful and act properly according to our position, social standing, environment, our education and vocation, using our body and speech in a good, clean way that has a pleasant effect upon others' perception; being very reasonable and acceptable. It is true that the most important thing is how we are inside but the outside is also very important because we are living in this world and should behave suitably.

### *c. Avoiding Narrow-Minded Practice*

Our devotion and compassion should not be biased. When we generate or cultivate devotion, it is towards our master, our teachers, the Buddhas, the Dharma teachings, the Lineage and so on but even though we have those principal foci we can still keep a very broad-minded approach that is open to all that is worthwhile. There are so many schools of Buddhism. Even just in Tibet there were nine main ones, latterly four, and even within one of those, the Kagyu-pa, there are fourteen sub-schools. Within one of those we follow a particular path, doing one technique and then the next, centred upon one line of practice. While in our particular evolutionary journey, we should remember that all the other schools are neither better nor worse than ours. They all have good foundations, paths and results; the Hinayana, Mahayana and Vajrayana aspects of practice. Even though we practice one in particular we must have respect for all the others since a sectarian attitude is so bad. We have to be non-sectarian but this does not mean mixing everything up and trying to do everything together; that will not work. We need to start with one thing and carry it through to its conclusion, all the time maintaining a respectful and healthy attitude towards the others.

This approach is very easy. Other religions also deserve our respect and we should avoid saying anything bad of them. They each constitute a path, complete in itself from its beginning to its end, and those paths are ways not just of a few but of millions: Christian, Hindu, Jewish, Islam and other great religions have brought much benefit and result to their followers. There is no point feeling bad or involved with them; life is too short to study them all, practice them all...it would end up a waste of time. One practice is enough; one path with a respect for all the others.

Compassion also deserves a broad-minded approach. It is easy to feel compassion towards other humans; every day we see the news on television and read the newspapers and there are so many murders, accidents etc. that the presence of distress before us will ever evoke our compassion. There is more than just that however. The animal realm is being eaten up by us all the time, not to mention the fact that we have enslaved it. Animals also have minds just like us and we need to feel for them also; likewise for the gods, asuras, pretas and hell-beings. There exists much more than just what we can see and touch. According to karmic causality, the mind creates the various sorts of body through the four elements, principally water and earth. Our compassion can embrace all the various beings in their different realms. Furthermore, ultimate compassion extends to all those under the sway of ego; we benefit them all. Through such an outlook, Mind Training cultivates devotion and compassion free of bias or narrowness.

There is also a ninefold way of presenting the above:

1. *To maintain a serious interest*: we avoid only being interested in what is new and fascinating. Having started any technique of Mind Training, it is to be carried through to the end and not simply dropped because of boredom. There is not much benefit in being superficial.
2. *To be exceedingly modest*: if we do manage to achieve any good thing then we just keep quiet about it, hiding it away. This is how to keep to very meaningful action, rather than virtuous action which is only an external mask, and how to avoid egotistic thoughts that arise when others praise our good works.
3. *Never to blame others:* Everyone makes mistakes, some more some less, but everyone makes them. This is not because the nature of all things is basically evil but because they are influenced to a greater or lesser extent by ignorance and because they are the slaves of ego. The more they are the slaves of ego, the more they will do what is negative. However, even the worst of them have some goodness deep down and do not always intend to do the bad that others see superficially. Our attitude towards all beings should be based upon helping them; it is never right to speak badly of others and it is very wrong to give others a bad reputation. Guarding our physical, verbal and mental activities very carefully, we always try to be compassionate and understanding, no matter what silly, nasty or strange things we see them do.
4. *To be without expectation or limited motivation:* Even though our general motivation is that of wishing to achieve realization in order to benefit beings, there is no need to constantly contrive each action, thinking, 'I am doing this in order to get this or that short or long-term result'. Just do the receiving-and-giving practice or any of the Mind Training techniques without expectation.
5. *Non-involvement with worldly activities:* We have to live and gain our livelihood, care for all those things which depend upon our care; but we should never let that get to the point where it becomes an involvement and increases egotism.

6. *Non-retaliation:* Even when someone has wronged us, never follow the initial thought of revenge, the dark and antagonistic feeling towards that person. Since we are applying the aspiration Bodhicitta and we belong to the Mahayana, we must give up any physical, verbal or mental retaliation.
7. *Acceptance of necessary difficulties:* There are some negative conditions which are unavoidable. When they occur, we have to accept them without trying to unload them onto others. When the difficult things have to be done then we should see them as our responsibility and it is not good to cause others suffering because we are unwilling to assume such responsibility.
8. *Full acceptance of the negative:* To behave selflessly without such mental tricks as thinking that by accepting the worst role now we will get the best one later.
9. *To avoid pride:* What we are doing in the Mind Training exercises is a very basic and simple thing: to train our motivation and thereby develop compassion. If we feel proud of our Mind Training in the sense of feeling better than others, then within that simple thing lies hidden the might of ego ; that has to be reduced as much as possible.

This chapter of the Mind Training is normally in fifteen points, which have been summed up here as nine for the sake of simplicity.

## Seventh Point - The Mind Training Precepts

This section usually contains many aspects of advice showing the correct way of practice implied by Mind Training and these have been grouped into the principal categories for convenience.

**1. The Three Difficulties**:
a. When we encounter an obstacle we have to understand it, and that is fairly difficult. It means being able to recognize the presence of the

poisons and their influence, and requires an initial awareness.
b. Having recognized its presence, we must then turn away from it.
c. Just turning away is not enough; we have to get rid of it forever.

In other words one needs recognition of the poison, use of antidote and a firm resolution to counteract it once and for all.

**2. The Three Prime Conditions to be Ever-Developed:**
a. The correct result will be achieved only by following the correct path and therefore we need right guidance (that of a master upon whom one can rely).
b. Our own insight and comprehension must be sufficiently strong.
c. We also need favourable circumstances to be able to apply the above.

Some people have these three prime conditions, some do not. If we do happen to have them then they should be put to the best possible use. If we do not have them, then there is nothing wrong with us - it just means that our understanding has not yet progressed enough. When these three prime conditions are not present there is no way that we can just create them.

**3. The Three Vital Factors Never to be Damaged:**
a. constant respect for and devotion towards the Mind Training practice,
b. great joy and confidence in applying it and
c. constant awareness of motivation on the inner level and of action on the outer level.

**Mind Training Should be the Constant Companion of:**
a. our body - the source of all action,
b. our speech - the source of expression and
c. our mind - the creator of thoughts.

**5. The Abandoning of Six Wrong Approaches in Favour of Six Right Ones:**

The first concerns *wrong patience and diligence.* Because of the power of ignorance, anything worthwhile always requires a lot of effort whereas the destructive or the negative is usually quite easy; for instance, to build a house requires so much time, money and labour yet it can be destroyed in just a few minutes. Worldly life being as it is, we have to have a fair amount of patient acceptance and sometimes persistence in order to be able to accomplish the relatively trivial and ordinary ambitions of our lives. Because we are still the slaves of egotism, any power of forbearance or diligence that we ordinarily have is that which is needed for these tasks and therefore it is wrong patience, wrong diligence, since it only serves to further what is samsaric. When the worthwhile meaningful tasks lie before us, we quickly tire of them and become bored. Abandoning the perpetuation of triviality caused by wrong diligence or patience, we need to re-channel their power towards the higher goals.

The second is to *abandon misguided aspiration.* Although most of us have a natural inclination to the right teachings etc. through our fortunate karma, there are many in this world whose main object of pursuit is relative happiness and glory.We need to stop chasing the supposed 'big things' of this life and turn attention to the great happiness that transcends the happiness-and-suffering of the relative world and that emerges with realization. Right aspiration is to wish for, pray for, the accomplishment of that.

The third is to *abandon 'wrong tasting'*, the flavour of the relative that is ever in our mouth, in favour of a developing taste for the savour of the ultimate. Through this there will be less wastage of our powers.

Fourth is to *abandon wrong compassion.* We must have compassion - of course, but sometimes it is the wrong compassion wherein we feel too much sympathy for those developing compassion themselves - the yogis. They can undergo so much - too much- and we feel so sorry for them but not for those who are afflicting them. Generally we are inclined to feel that way. If, for instance, a very cruel person, powerful and selfish, is torturing others then we naturally feel compassion for his victims much more than for him. We should sympathise with those who are suffering, but even more with those who create their sufferings simply because of the nature of karma.

Fifth is to *abandon wrong striving.* We who are in the Dharma have a little understanding of the way things are; we try not to be too proud of it and to increase it as much as possible. We all want the very best for our friends and family, but it is no good striving for those loved ones if what we are doing is basically increasing their negative karma. Sometimes, for instance, we see parents who, like all parents, want the best for their children but who, through their ignorance, just make life worse for them. Instead of that sort of thing, we should lead those we want to help only in the right direction; otherwise we are not helping them at all. So we educate our children with a view to making them the best people with the very best understanding. There is little more to be said - it is very obvious to sensitive people.

Sixth is to *abandon wrong rejoicing*. If anyone, even our enemy, is happy, we should' rejoice in', feel a sympathetic joy in, his happiness. Chairman Mao was very catastrophic for Tibet; through him many evils were perpetrated. When he died many Tibetans held celebrations, picnics and rejoiced. That was very bad! Buddhists should not do that. That someone be truly on the way to deeper understanding is a very special cause for our rejoicing.

The above advice is directly from the Mind Training scriptures. There are some general guidelines that are also very useful in helping us understand life and its meaning:

1. Before doing any practice, clarify any confusion about it.
2. When all doubt and confusion has been removed, practice without laziness, not necessarily working twenty-four hours a day at it, but always being aware of it whatever is happening, even if just lying around doing nothing. Such mindfulness of the teachings' meaning is real diligence.
3. Don't do anything casually: first think about it, find out about it. When sure about it, do it and finish it, finishing the earlier undertakings first and the later ones last.
4. Always discipline body, speech and mind with awareness and mindfulness. Until now the ego has been the king and you its slave and it always led in the wrong direction. From today onwards, turn the ego into a good king; if you must be its slave then at least let the situation be beneficial, for yourself and all beings. There are many ways of disciplining body, speech and mind:

* Abandon all harshness in physical, verbal and mental actions, cultivating all that leads to peace.
* Avoid negative livelihood; gain food, clothing, name or fame in a

wholesome way. If there are two people eating similar bread and one earns it by working for a world peace organization, by cleaning or anything wholesome while the other earned his money as a slaughterer, then the former's money was pure and the latter's impure.
* In public keep a check on body, speech and mind, constantly. In private keep a check on the mind. Publicly we can create bad karma by negative speech and physical actions; by ourselves at home, saying bad things does not mean very much - it is the mind that needs checking.
* Generally, always keep well away from the ten non-virtues and stick firmly to the ten virtues.

Further advice is to continually develop compassion, in particular:

* to feel for all beings as a mother feels for her only child; as that child feels for its mother. It sounds almost impossible but can be achieved by gradually stepping up the power of *tong.len,* the giving-and-accepting meditation. The 'I' who gives and receives is only one person; the 'others' who benefit from this are all those beings throughout the galaxy. Since they outnumber 'me' so greatly, then anything 'I' can give that is likely to benefit them should be given. This means giving our happiness and causes of happiness to **all** beings.
* negative circumstances are our very best teachers. Through them we come to understand the sufferings of samsara; without that understanding we would be samsara's slaves forever. A suffering that we have to undergo in this life is not a punishment. It had a cause which is being annihilated by the suffering itself and that suffering can be further used (in tong.len for instance) as something positive. There is no time to be wasted or no such opportunity to be missed. Instead of getting depressed and feeling bad about suffering we can take it as part of the path to realization.

Finally at all times, day or night, conscious or dreaming, to keep the *tong.len* attitude ever-present. With it, always doing our best and being free of fear and self-pity, we will not be afraid or feel lost even if we were to die this very minute.

The Mind Training ends with a mention of the *Seven Treasures of the Realized.* Ordinary worldly wealth, even that of a king, lasts at the most for only one life. The good times and happiness cannot be taken across the threshold of death - not one servant, not even a grain of rice. All that can accompany one is mental conditioning. The Seven Treasures of Realized Beings are:

1. faith and confidence in our motivation and the objects of devotion,
2. pure conduct,
3. dedication of virtue,
4. an accumulation of knowledge, of clear and total understanding,
5. self-respect related to a wholesome sense of the shameful,
6. dignity related to a sane sense of embarrassment and
7. the wisdom that comprehends the ultimate truth.

These seven inestimable wealths are accumulated by the techniques and practices of Mind Training.

I am sure that we shall all derive great benefit through what we already know and through what we are studying. Maybe some of us already have the confidence that truth brings, even now in this life. If not, then we will have it some day. Let there be no more fear or self-pity.

## Author's Dedication

*Beside any immediate benefit of understanding that this book may bring to the reader, may its virtue speed the swift return of my teacher, His Holiness the Gyalwa Karmapa, among us and make His teaching long and without obstacle. May it also bring long life and sustenance to all the Dharma-Teachers and Dharma-helpers, strengthening their work and freeing them from hindrances. Through it, may peace and goodness spread throughout the universe.*